W9-BVX-190

Hooked on Seafood

Annette Reddell Hegen
Seafood Consumer Education Specialist
Texas Marine Advisory Service

Best wishes for lots of good seafood dishes! Annette

A TEXAS A&M SEA GRANT PUBLICATION

Publication of this book supported in part by Institutional Grant Number NA16RG0457-01 to Texas A&M University Sea Grant College Program from the National Sea Grant Program, National Oceanic and Atmospheric Administration, U.S. Department of Commerce. The Texas Marine Advisory Service is a cooperative effort of the Sea Grant College Program, the Texas Agricultural Extension Service, Texas Parks and Wildlife Department and the commercial fisheries' industry of Texas.

Food Photographer—Ron Randolph, Ron Randolph Photography, Corpus Christi
Food Stylist—Annette Reddell Hegen
Book Editing and Design—Amy Broussard

Texas A&M University Sea Grant College Program
Publication TAMU-SG-93-501
ISBN 1-883550-00-9

For more information on Texas A&M Sea Grant publications, contact:
        Sea Grant Program
        Texas A&M University
        P.O. Box 1675
        Galveston, Texas 77553-1675

Dedication

Dedicated to those members of the commercial seafood industry who work endless hours under tiring and stressful conditions to supply us with wonderful seafood products; and to conscientious processors, wholesalers and retailers who do their part in the marketing channel to offer a product that makes us heroes at mealtime.

Preface

The Texas A&M University Sea Grant College Program is pleased to present to you this collection of Texas' finest seafood recipes.

These recipes have all been tested, evaluated and retested. Many have been distributed through retail markets throughout the country, and used in countless media events and in presentations to the general public and various professional audiences. Some are favorite seafood recipes from the best seafood chefs in Texas, as noted by their participation in the Texas Seafood Challenge, an annual seafood cooking competition for professional chefs. One or two were even gently persuaded from reluctant coastal restuaranteurs who protect their best recipes with unwavering loyalty.

As new concepts in nutrition emerge, I have developed recipes and revised old ones to make them more heart healthy. If you are truly on a restrictive diet, feel free to add, delete or substitute ingredients in these recipes to make them fit your diet requirements. You will notice that, in most cases, particular species are not indicated on the recipes. Varieties of fish are interchangeable. Use the good quality products available in your area to create a seafood appetizer, accompaniment dish or entree from these suggestions. Best wishes for lots of good seafood dishes prepared in the comfort of your own home!

—Annette Reddell Hegen

Table of Contents

Why Seafood?

Seafood is a wonderful food. At its finest, it is firm or flaky in texture, mild or distinct in flavor, white, pink, gray or brown in color, and comes in a myriad of shapes. There is no other food category like it. With seafood, you have hundreds of choices.

But what really is so special about seafood? It is quick to fix, easy to cook, high in protein, low in fat, low in sodium, a great source of calcium and an excellent source of omega-3 fatty acids, which appear to lower cholesterol and reduce the risk of heart disease. In addition to all that, it tastes good!

No doubt about it. We're a nation hooked on fish. At our rate of consumption, we should reach 20 pounds per capita by the year 2000! If this should happen, though, an additional 2.6 billion pounds of whole fish and shellfish will be required to fill the demand. Most of this will come from aquacultured products.

Ready...set...go!

Beginners of fish cookery, get ready to acquire a habit you won't want to break. You can learn to cook seafoods indoors or outdoors. Listen to the sizzling fish, sniff the mouth-watering aroma of freshly grilled fish or shellfish, and enjoy the good company of friends and family. You will delight in the exceptional flavor and texture of seafood flavored with mesquite or hickory wood smoke and cooked over the coals. Why not organize a fishing trip to the retail market and let the grand finale be a soiree utilizing the results of your "fishing" efforts? Or, if you are a sport fisherman, experiment with species that you have previously just wondered about or even thrown back. Yes, using non-traditional species is in vogue. What was once considered to be trash or rough fish now commands high prices at fine restaurants and rates high in the flavor department, too.

The best way to catch fish in a store.

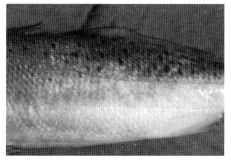

Observe Eyes and Gills: *Fresh fish have clear, bright, protruding eyes and reddish gills. A fish with clouded or sunken eyes, or slimy grey, greenish or brownish gills is not acceptable.*

Check for Color and Sheen: *The shiny iridescent luster and distinct coloration of freshly caught fish fade gradually. Reject fish that appear dull, slimy or washed-out.*

Take a Sniff: *The better the fish, the fresher it will smell. A "fishy" odor is a sign of aging. Choose fish with a mild, oceany scent. Reject any that have a disagreeably strong odor.*

**Scratch and Press:** *The scales of high quality fish will adhere tightly to the skin when scratched. The flesh is firm and springs back when touched. Flakey scales or spongy flesh indicate spoiling.*

**Fresh in the Shell:** *Shellfish must be alive to be fresh. Crabs should be active. Mussels, clams and oysters should feel heavy and be tightly closed, or close immediately when handled.*

Freshly Shucked: *Shucked oysters, clams and scallops must be completely covered in their own liquid, iced or re-frigerated immediately and eaten soon after purchase. Clouded liquid and an ammonia-like odor indicates spoilage.*

What's Good?

Whole Fish — Look for firm, translucent flesh, a red gill area, clear bulging eyes, pink or red belly area, a just-caught look and a pleasant, fresh (or non-existent) odor. Ice fish down as soon as you buy or catch it.

Shrimp — High quality shrimp should be free of discoloration or freezer burn. The head is usually securely attached to the tail if whole, although sometimes the head can become loose while being caught or when stirred with ice at the retail level. Shrimp will have a fresh clean odor.

Oysters — Recently shucked oysters will have a clean odor with no ammonia smell, a thin clear liquid, plump body and be free of extraneous material. Oysters in the shell should be alive. The shells will be tightly closed or will close when tapped.

Crabs — Blue crabs should be lively if uncooked and reddish-orange in color and chilled if cooked. Picked meat will be chilled or frozen and free of excess shell and cartilage. The flavor is sweet and the odor is mild.

Frozen items — Frozen items should be solidly frozen. Avoid products with freezer burn and ice crystals visible under the wrapper. Also avoid fish that has yellowed, which is an indication of rancidity or oxidation of fats. The technology of handling seafood has improved tremendously in recent years. Commercially frozen fish has been quickly frozen at its peak and the consumer can now find a wide choice of top quality and wholesome seafood in the freezer case. Do not allow the package to defrost during transportation.

All seafoods are highly perishable. Make your seafood purchase the last one before returning home. Carrying a small ice chest or cooler with you on your grocery shopping trip will help reduce the chance of quality loss. To keep seafood in peak condition, maintain cold temperature at all times before cooking to keep the product in peak condition. Keep seafood in the coldest part of your refrigerator or freeze it until ready to use. This is vital to the final outcome of your dish. The danger zone is 40 to 160 degrees F.

Boning Up

The secret to cooking fish properly is to cook it only until it's done. Because there is so little connective tissue, fish cooks quickly at moderate heat. One suggestion is to cook the fish 10 minutes per inch of thickness measured at its thickest part. It is better to undercook the fish and then check for doneness. Cook it longer if necessary. Fish is done when the flesh is opaque and it flakes easily. Juices should still be apparent. Fish cooked too long will have relinquished much flavor and moisture, resulting in an inferior product.

Fish market forms

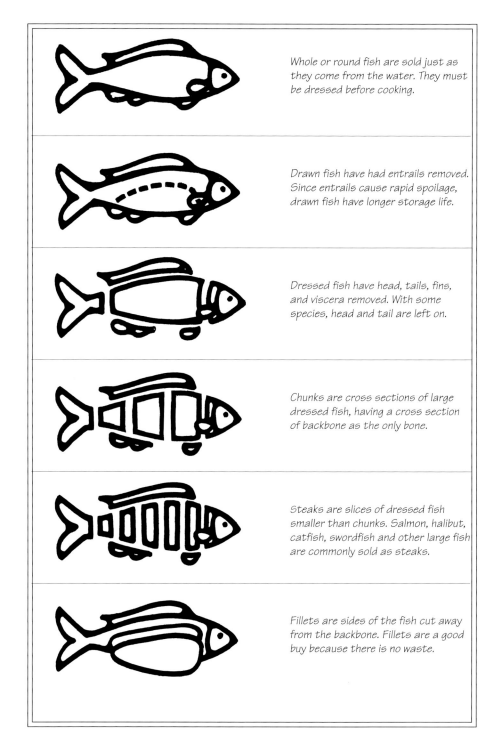

Whole or round fish are sold just as they come from the water. They must be dressed before cooking.

Drawn fish have had entrails removed. Since entrails cause rapid spoilage, drawn fish have longer storage life.

Dressed fish have head, tails, fins, and viscera removed. With some species, head and tail are left on.

Chunks are cross sections of large dressed fish, having a cross section of backbone as the only bone.

Steaks are slices of dressed fish smaller than chunks. Salmon, halibut, catfish, swordfish and other large fish are commonly sold as steaks.

Fillets are sides of the fish cut away from the backbone. Fillets are a good buy because there is no waste.

Start with the Basics

Baking

   This is a dry heat method of cooking that works for just about any kind of fish in any market form. Prepare a baking pan with a nonstick vegetable spray or a small amount of oil. The fish can be placed on lemon slices to add flavor and prevent sticking. Place the fillets on the pan, skin side down, even if skinless. Bake at 350 degrees until the fish is opaque but still juicy, about 10 minutes per inch of thickness. For thin fillets you will need to baste or use a bread or cracker topping, sauce or liquid to prevent drying. Anne Fletcher, author of **Eat Fish, Live Better**, suggests topping baked fish with lemon juice and herbs. If the fish needs a bit more moisture a tablespoon of melted margarine, butter or oil will do for four people and can be stretched by mixing with several tablespoons of lemon or lime juice. Bread crumbs and crushed crackers or flake-type cereals can be used as tasty toppings that help seal in moisture. Fish can also be baked by wrapping in foil.

Broiling

   This is an intense dry heat method in which the fish is placed about 4 inches below the heat source. Fish is well suited for broiling because it cooks quickly and is naturally tender. Any variety of fish can be broiled, but fish with a high oil content require no additional fat or sauce as they are somewhat self-basting. A splash of lemon or lime juice is always tasty.

Grilling

   Cooking seafood on the outdoor grill is easy and creates a flavor unlike any-thing you can create indoors. A metal grill over direct heat can be used for cooking seafood. Follow the procedure suggested by your appliance manufacturer and remember these two points. First, begin with a good quality product. Poorly handled fish will produce an unacceptable grilled item. Second, use moderate heat, turning the product only if grilling very thick fish. Seafood items should be at least 4 to 6 inches from the heat source. To retain natural juices and fine flavor, be careful not to overcook the product. From hibachis to covered units with motor-ized spits, Texas seafoods cooked over the coals offer a festive alternative to conventional cooking.

Microwaving

   To cook fish via microwaves, it is important to follow the guidelines from your manufacturer and to practice with simple fish dishes. Dr. Joyce Nettleton in

Seafood and Health says it is impossible to give exact cooking times for microwaving fish, because the power of different ovens varies with the make and model. Cooking time varies with the power of the oven, the density and thickness of the fish and other ingredients and the amount you are cooking. Microwave cooking times are one-fourth to one-third of those used for conventional recipes. The recipes in this book were developed for conventional cooking methods. With a little experimentation, you can adapt them to microwave cookery.

Poaching

This method involves cooking the fish in a small amount of a seasoned liquid, such as a stock or courtbouillon (*koo be yawn*). The fish is cooked gently at just below the boiling point in the oven or on the stove top. A courtbouillon is a broth made by cooking various vegetables and herbs in water for about 30 minutes. Wine, lemon juice or vinegar may be added. After the seafood is poached, it can be served as is, with a sauce or flaked and added to a variety of recipes for salads, dips or spreads.

Sauteing or Pan Frying

Seafoods can be cooked quickly in a small amount of oil in a skillet over direct heat. Fish is often sautéed or seared and then finished in the oven. When other ingredients are included, the method is called "stir-fry."

Stir Frying

This cooking technique is associated with oriental cooking. It requires a minimum amount of oil and high heat and results in a food that is crispy tender.

Barbecuing

Seafoods cooked by barbecuing are covered and slowly cooked in a pit using hot coals or hardwood as a heat source. A highly seasoned sauce is used to keep the fish or shellfish moist.

How to dress a fish for dinner.

Dressed for stuffing.

Scale the fish, moving the scaler from the tail to the head. Be sure to remove the scales close to the fins. Scaling can be done with a fish scaler, a knife or even a tablespoon.

Open the belly cavity by making a straight cut from the anal opening to the jaw. Scrape out the internal organs with your knife.

Be sure to remove any blood along the backbone of the fish. Cut out the gills with a knife or a pair of kitchen shears. Wash the fish thoroughly with cold running water. The fish is now ready to stuff.

Filleting.

  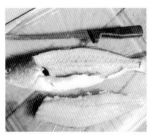

Scale the fish (unless you intend to skin the fillet). Make a diagonal cut behind the pectoral fin toward the head. Cut down until you feel the backbone. It helps to have a filleting knife or other knife with a sharp, thin blade.

Make a shallow cut from head to tail just above the dorsal fin. Carefully cut the fillet off by running the knife just on top of the backbone. To have a boneless fillet, avoid cutting into the belly cavity or, if you cut into the belly cavity, remove the rib bones by sliding your knife just underneath them and cutting them off diagonally.

The fillet is now ready to be prepared in the way you like best.

Steaking.

Steaking is common for catfish, tuna, swordfish, or salmon. Cut off the head, remove the internal organs, and wash in cold water to remove any blood and remaining viscera.

Make a cut perpendicular to the backbone, about one inch from the head end. If you have trouble with this cut, tap the knife with a hammer.

Make perpendicular cuts at one inch intervals down the length of the fish. The "steaks" are now ready to grill, bake or prepare in your favorite way.

Interchangeability

It is helpful to know the oil content, density and texture of fish when selecting a product for a recipe. Then you know what to expect in terms of flakiness, intensity of flavor and stability. Feel free to experiment with different species in these recipes as I did. I didn't indicate a particular one on most recipes for fear beginning cooks would be hesitant to use anything but the one indicated.

Lean — These are fish with less than 2 percent fat and are suitable in recipes that involve added moisture. Recipes with toppings, sauces, creoles, soups and salad are good choices for these fish. They can also be cooked by a dry heat method but may need basting. All shellfish are lean.

cod	pike
dolphinfish (mahi mahi)	pollock
drum	rockfish
flounder	sheepshead
haddock	sole
hake	snapper
monkfish	whiting
perch	

Medium — These fish have 2.1 to 5 percent fat and are suitable for any method of cooking. The fish is fairly firm and maintains its shape while cooking.

bass	smelt
catfish	swordfish
croaker	tilefish
halibut	trout
orange roughy	tuna
pompano	turbot
shark	

Fat — These fish have more than 5 percent fat and are great for grilling, baking or broiling because of their stability.

anchovies	mackerels
bonito	mullet
butterfish	sablefish
carp	salmon
herring	shad

Eating Out

Anne M. Fletcher, a registered dietitian, consultant and free-lance writer, is a frequent seafood industry spokesperson. She offers these tips for enjoying fish in restaurants without sacrificing nutrition.

- Ask for fish and shellfish to be poached, steamed, broiled, grilled or baked with little or no added fat.
- Be assertive, asking for sauces and dressings on the side.
- Order tomato-based soups instead of cream-based chowders.
- Seek the American Heart Association-approved menu items for low-calorie and saturated fat entree alternatives.
- Dine out at lunchtime or take advantage of less expensive early-bird specials.
- Use dining out experiences to taste-test new and unusual fish that you might be less willing to try for the first time at home.
- Reject any food item that is not satisfactory in quality or is not prepared as you asked.

Approximate Cholesterol/Calorie Content of Finfish per 3 1/2 Ounces Raw Edible Weight*

Species	Cholesterol mg	Calories
Atlantic Cod	43	82
Butterfish	65	146
Carp	66	127
Croaker	60	104
Dolphinfish	73	85
Drum, freshwater	64	119
Eel	125	184
Flounder, sole	50	91
Grouper	37	92
Haddock	65	87
Halibut	32	110
Herring	60	158
Ling	—	87
Mackerel, king	53	105
Mackerel, Spanish	76	139
Monkfish	25	76
Mullet, striped	49	117
Orange roughy	20	126
Perch, ocean	42	94
Pollock	71	81
Pompano	50	164
Red snapper	37	100
Salmon, chum	75	180
Salmon, sockeye	62	168
Seatrout	83	104
Shark	51	130
Sheepshead	—	126
Surimi	30	99
Swordfish	39	121
Tilefish	—	96
Trout	58	148
Tuna, bluefin	38	144
Tuna, canned in oil	37	198
Tuna, canned in water	—	131
Tuna, yellowfin	45	108
Whitefish	60	184
Whiting	28	90

*Data from USDA Composition of Food, #8-15; 1987.

A Healthy Choice

Seafood has come a long way since the tradition of eating fish on Fridays was so popular. People are enjoying fish for the taste, ease and versatility of preparation and for its outstanding nutritional qualities.

Although seafood is popular for all these reasons, the nutritional benefits probably account for the current and steady increase in consumption.

Omega-3 Fatty Acids

What is omega-3 fatty acid? This refers to the unique chemical structure of the fatty acids found in many plants and animals from the sea. It has been found that eating large amounts of omega-3 fatty acids can decrease the tendency of blood platelet cells, involved with clotting, to stick or clump together. This decreases the likelihood of forming clots that can block blood flow to the heart and result in a heart attack. According to Dr. William P. Castelli, medical director for the Framingham Heart Study, "Fish should be put up above everything else on the diet because they can actually reverse the process of arterial damage that leads to heart attacks."

Both freshwater and marine species have omega-3 fatty acids. Fattier species from both environments are the richest sources of omega-3 fatty acids. Generally, these are recognizable by their dark flesh. Since the omega-3 fatty acids come from the green plant material in the water, fish fed naturally from the environment have higher levels than farm-raised fish, unless the fish food is supplemented with omega-3s. Providing omega-3 fatty acids in aquaculture for the well-being of the fish and the people who eat them is an important consideration in today's fish technology.

Protein

The protein in seafood compares favorably with chicken, beef, eggs and cheese for top honors in supplying us with all the amino acids we need for tissue building and repair. That makes it an efficient source of protein for meeting our basic needs. The protein in seafood is easily digested and is essential to our health through all stages of the life cycle. One serving of fish will give you half of the protein you need all day.

Vitamins

Seafood is an important source of several B vitamins essential for good health. They assist in the processing of energy coming from the foods we eat. Many seafoods, especially dark-fleshed species such as mackerel and bluefish, are the richest sources of these vitamins. Other B vitamins in seafood are used to metabolize amino acids from protein, obtain cellular energy from carbohydrates and are required for healthy red blood cells.

Minerals

Seafoods are rich in iron, calcium and phosphorus. Clams, mussels and oysters are especially rich sources of iron. Eating a variety of seafoods on a regular basis can do a great deal to boost iron values, particularly necessary for women. Anchovies, periwinkles, tuna and freshwater catfish head the list of rich sources of magnesium, which is an important mineral for bone metabolism. Minerals needed in small amounts, but vital for a variety of body functions, are called trace minerals. Fluorine, iodine, zinc, copper and selenium are found in all marine seafood products. Seafoods are low in sodium and are excellent choices for people on a sodium-restricted diet.

Fat

Seafoods contain a high proportion of polyunsaturated fat, the kind that keeps blood vessels healthy. Most fish have less than 5 percent fat, while all shellfish have less than 2 percent fat. The fat in seafood is beneficial to our health. All shellfish is considered lean.

Approximate Cholesterol/Calorie Content of Shellfish per 3 1/2 Ounces Raw Edible Weight*

Mollusks	Cholesterol mg	Calories
Abalone	85	105
Clams, mixed species	34	74
Mussels	28	86
Octopus	48	82
Oysters	50	69
Scallops, mixed species	35	88
Squid, mixed species	250	92
Crustaceans	Cholesterol mg	Calories
Crab, blue	72	87
Crab, dungeness	60	86
Crab, king	42	84
Crawfish	170	85
Lobster, spiny	80	112
Rock Shrimp	121	90
Shrimp	150	106

*Data from USDA Composition of Food, #8-15, 1987; Dr. S.W. Otwell, Extension Seafood Specialist, University of Florida.

Safety First

Seafood is no exception when it comes to the importance of handling and preparing foods properly to minimize the risk of food-borne illness. Actually, seafood is the cause of human illness only when

- it comes from contaminated waters and you eat it raw.
- you eat it raw and it has spoiled because of improper handling.
- it spoils because it has not been handled properly either by the fisherman, the dealer, the restaurant or you at home.
- it spoils because there is damage to the package and bacteria has gotten in.
- it contains toxins produced by or found naturally in that species of fish.
- you are allergic to the seafood and you inhale fumes from that species of seafood, either raw or cooked. Food poisoning is often mistaken for food allergy.
- it contains certain parasites that have not been destroyed because it is served raw or lightly cured.

Seafood Safeguards

To guard against food-borne illness and to help ensure a good quality product, follow these tips.

Know your seafood retailer. Buy seafood products from approved licensed stores and markets. Establish a friendly rapport, so you aren't sold second best. Better yet, shop where only top quality products are sold.

Purchase raw shellfish carefully. Buy raw oysters, clams and mussels only from approved, reputable sources. If in doubt, ask the seafood market personnel to show you the certified shipper's tag that accompanies "shell-on" products or check the shipper information on shucked oyster containers. Shell-stocked products must be alive when purchased. Do not accept dead oysters, mussels or clams unless they are cooked or the meat is shucked and chilled.

Keep seafoods cold. Keep fresh, pasteurized or smoked seafood products refrigerated at 32 to 34 degrees F. Since most of our home refrigerators are set higher than that, store seafood "on the rocks." Wrap it tightly in a plastic wrap or securely in a plastic container and place ice above and below it. Freeze it if you do not use it within two days.

Refrigerate live shellfish properly. Live shellfish, such as clams, mussels and oysters should be stored in well-ventilated refrigeration, not in airtight plastic bags or containers. Live lobsters and crabs should also be stored in a well-ventilated area. Cover them with damp paper towels in the refrigerator.

Keep live shellfish alive. Do not cook or eat shellfish such as lobsters, crabs, clams, oysters or mussels if they have died during storage. Discard them.

Don't cross contaminate. Handle raw and cooked seafood products separately. Thoroughly clean and rinse the work space between each step. This also includes cleaning the knives, containers and cutting boards used during preparation. Plexiglas or plastic cutting boards are preferred over wooden ones that cannot be sanitized properly. Keep raw and cooked seafoods from coming in contact with each other.

Cook fish and shellfish thoroughly. Fish is cooked when it turns opaque and reaches an internal temperature of 145 degrees F. Follow processors' directions when preparing frozen, packaged seafood products.

Eating your own catch is rewarding. Make sure the waters from which you fish are approved for harvest. Check with your state or local health department or law enforcement agency that oversees fishing regulations.

Eating Raw Oysters

The Food and Drug Administration (FDA) has advised that individuals with chronic liver disease or compromised immune systems should avoid consuming raw or partially cooked oysters. A common saltwater microorganism, *Vibrio vulnificus*, is occasionally carried by oysters, especially in summer months in Gulf coast waters. It can be the cause of severe illness or death for individuals with such medical conditions as:

- liver disease, including cirrhosis and hemochromatosis
- chronic alcohol abuse
- cancer, especially if taking anti-cancer drugs or radiation treatment
- compromised immune systems
- diabetes mellitus
- chronic kidney disease
- inflammatory bowel disease
- steroid dependency
- achlorhydria (a condition in which the normal acidity of the stomach is reduced or absent)

Since the microorganism is destroyed by heat, consumers with these conditions are advised to enjoy all seafoods in their many delicious, cooked preparations.

Freezing Seafoods

Fish should be frozen to eliminate air and in package sizes to accommodate one meal. I suggest freezing fish fillets individually by wrapping each fillet in a cling wrap and pressing out all air pockets. Then place several of these in a freezer bag and force all the air.

Shrimp should be headed and rinsed under cold water. Pack the shrimp with ice in containers sized for your family. Fill with water, leaving a little space for expansion. Leaving the shell on provides extra insulation against freezer burn.

Crab meat can be frozen although it does undergo some textural and flavor changes. Pack it tightly in airtight containers. If you want to prepare live crab for freezing, consider processing and freezing just the core. The core is the main body area, cleaned and without legs attached. Deback, clean and wash the crab. Then boil and freeze it. Rapid cooling is essential, so individual cores should be wrapped and frozen, or frozen and glazed as rapidly as possible before being wrapped in a larger package.

Oysters previously frozen may be disappointing to you. It is almost impossible to avoid textural changes during frozen storage. However, with proper handling and freezing techniques, these changes are not severe, especially if the oysters are to be cooked. Place shucked oysters and natural liquor in a container and fill with water leaving one inch of air space at the top. Another method is to fill small zip-lock freezer bags with oysters and liquid. Zip shut, eliminating all air space. Thaw in the bag in cold water or in the refrigerator.

Thawing Seafoods

Thawing in cold water is the fastest and best means of thawing. Proper thawing is just as important as proper freezing. Improper thawing can greatly reduce the quality of the seafood product. As a rule, seafoods should be thawed as quickly as possible, but never in hot water or at room temperature. Slow thawing in a refrigerator causes excessive drip loss and can give spoilage bacteria time to produce off-odors and off-flavors. It could take 12 to 18 hours for a 2- to 4-pound fish to thaw in a refrigerator. Thawing at room temperature can create uneven thawing and cause thin sections to spoil before the thicker portions thaw. Thawing in hot water greatly denatures the proteins and creates excessive loss of moisture and flavor. Seafoods can be thawed successfully in a microwave oven on the lowest setting if done right before preparation. Seafoods can be cooked frozen, but extra cooking time is needed. For highest quality, keep seafoods frozen until defrosting them for use. If frozen seafoods thaw before needed, they may be refrozen if ice crystals are still present. The quality may deteriorate slightly after freezing, but the product will be safe to eat.

Ceviche, page 19

Oyster and Mushroom Soup

When I serve this as a preamble to a special meal it sets the stage for success! The delicious broth with cream and sherry simply envelopes the oysters.

1 pint shucked oysters
1/2 cup coarsely chopped onion
4 tablespoons margarine
1 1/2 cups sliced mushrooms
3/4 cup chicken broth
1/4 teaspoon thyme

1/4 teaspoon each salt and pepper
1 tablespoon chopped chives
1 cup light cream
3/4 cup milk
1 tablespoon sherry or 1/4 cup dry
   white wine

In a large saucepan, saute onion in margarine until translucent. Add mushrooms and saute 2 to 3 minutes more. Add oysters, broth and heat without boiling until oysters curl. Stir in remaining ingredients and heat throughout. Makes 4 servings.

Fish and Vegetable Soup

This is a light and soothing soup—colorful and not detrimental to your waistline.

1 pound skinless fish fillets
6 cups chicken broth
1 cup sliced carrots
1 cup sliced fresh mushrooms
2 onions, cut into eighths
2 cups fresh broccoli florets
2 tablespoons cornstarch

1/2 teaspoon basil
1/2 teaspoon oregano
1/8 teaspoon pepper
1 peeled tomato, cut into 8 wedges
2 tablespoons sliced, pimiento-
   stuffed olives

Cut fish into 1-inch chunks. In a large stew pot, combine broth and vegetables. Cook on medium heat for 5 minutes, then reduce heat. Mix cornstarch with 1/4 cup water. Add to hot liquid, stirring gently while soup simmers. Add fish and remaining ingredients and cook for 5 to 8 minutes. Serve immediately with a crusty bread. Makes 8 servings.

Shrimp and Asparagus Soup

Combining the two special flavors of shrimp and asparagus in a soup is a great idea. Use a lighter milk product if you want to.

1 pound cooked shrimp or cooked,
   flaked fish
1 tablespoon margarine
1/2 cup long grain rice
1 small chopped onion
5 cups chicken broth

1 can (10 ounces) chopped asparagus
1/4 teaspoon grated nutmeg
Salt and pepper to taste
2 tablespoons fresh lemon juice
1 cup chilled whipping cream

Melt margarine in large saucepan. Stir in rice and onion and saute until rice is solid white, about 5 minutes. Add broth and bring to a boil. Reduce heat and simmer, stirring occasionally, about 30 minutes. Gently stir in remaining ingredients and heat throughout. Makes 6 servings.

Landlubber's Fish Stew

This stew is always a hit when I pass out samples at festivals and fairs.

1 pound shark steaks or fillets or
   other fish
3 strips bacon
1 cup chopped onion
2 cans (10 3/4 ounces each)
   condensed cream of potato soup
2 cups diluted evaporated or whole
   milk
1 can (1 pound) stewed tomatoes,
   slightly chopped

1 package (10 ounces) frozen mixed
   vegetables, thawed
1 package (10 ounces) whole kernel
   corn
1/2 teaspoon salt
1/8 teaspoon pepper
1 small bay leaf

Cut fish into chunks. In large stew pot, cook bacon until crisp. Remove bacon to absorbent paper and crumble. Cook onion in bacon drippings until tender. Add soup, milk, tomatoes, vegetables, corn, salt, pepper and bay leaf. Heat, stirring occasionally, until mixture simmers. Add fish and bacon and simmer about 10 minutes or until fish flakes and is opaque. Makes 9 cups chowder.

 To make a rich stock for gumbo, place shrimp heads, lemon slices and onions in a cheese cloth bag and boil in water.

Hot Fish Potato Salad

Use a firm fleshed fish like snapper, grouper or any big game fish for this family favorite.

1 pound fresh fish fillets, cut in 1-inch chunks
6 slices cooked and crumbled bacon, reserve grease
1/2 cup sliced celery
1/2 cup chopped onion
3 tablespoons sugar
1 tablespoon flour
1/2 teaspoon paprika
1/4 teaspoon salt
1/4 teaspoon celery seeds
1/2 cup wine vinegar
1 cup water
3 cups sliced cooked potatoes
Chopped fresh parsley

Saute celery and onion in bacon grease until tender. Combine sugar, flour, paprika, salt and celery seeds. Stir mixture into sauteed vegetables. Add vinegar and water gradually. Cook until thickened, stirring constantly. Add potatoes, bacon and fish and mix lightly. Cover and cook over low heat for 10 minutes or until fish flakes easily when tested with a fork. Sprinkle with parsley. Makes 6 servings.

Ceviche

Because food technologists and health professionals recommend we avoid eating raw seafood, this novel salad safely features tender pieces of cooked fish flavored with lime juice. The taste is the same as the original raw fish salad.

1 pound lean, white, skinless fish fillets
1/2 cup fresh lime juice
1/2 cup chopped onion
1 cup chopped tomatoes
1 small chopped jalapeno pepper
2 tablespoons chopped fresh parsley
30 pimiento stuffed olives
20 capers
1/4 cup olive oil
1/8 teaspoon cumin
Salt and pepper to taste
1/4 teaspoon oregano

Cut the fish into dime-size pieces. Place fish pieces in a skillet in enough water to cover and simmer for 3 minutes or until the fish is opaque. Drain and chill. In a refrigerator bowl with a sealable lid, place fish pieces and lime juice. Refrigerate for at least 4 hours, inverting once. Drain fish and mix with remaining ingredients. Makes 4 to 6 servings. (Pictured opposite page 16)

Fish Waldorf Salad

Fresh fish and a melange of fruits are featured in this main luncheon dish. I've served it with fresh shrimp, too.

2 cups cooked, coarsely flaked fish
1 cored and chopped apple
1 sliced banana
1 can (8 ounces) pineapple chunks, drained
1/2 cup raisins
1/2 cup chopped walnuts or pecans
1/2 cup plain yogurt, mayonnaise or sour cream
1 tablespoon lemon juice
Salad greens
Apple wedges for garnish

In a large mixing bowl, combine all ingredients except greens and apple wedges. Toss gently. Chill and serve on salad greens. Garnish with apple wedges. Makes 4 generous servings.

Escabeche

Of Spanish origin, this is a cold dish with cooked fish layered with vegetables and marinated up to 2 hours. I use a firm, dense-textured fish like ling, tuna, grouper or kingfish.

2 pounds firm fish, steaks or fillets
1/2 cup olive oil
4 onions, sliced in rings and halved
4 green bell peppers, cut julienne
4 minced garlic cloves
3 bay leaves
1/2 teaspoon paprika
1 cup pitted green olives
1/4 cup white vinegar
1/2 cup olive oil
Salt and pepper to taste

Sprinkle fish with salt and saute in oil over medium heat just until done, about 5 minutes. Drain on paper towels. Add onions and bell peppers to skillet and saute for 2 minutes. Add remaining ingredients and mix well. Remove from heat. In a glass dish, for visual appeal, alternate layers of fish then the vegetable mixture, ending with vegetables. Cover and refrigerate several hours or overnight. Remove from refrigerator 30 minutes before serving.

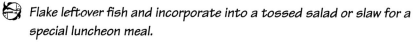 *Flake leftover fish and incorporate into a tossed salad or slaw for a special luncheon meal.*

Texas Sea Slaw

Take this along to a barbecue where a good slaw is expected. This one is colorful and a great way to get one of your heart healthy meals for the week.

1/2 pound each cooked chopped
  shrimp and flaked fish
3 cups chopped red cabbage
3 cups chopped green cabbage
1/2 cup grated carrots

1/4 cup snipped fresh parsley
1 cup "lite" mayonnaise
1 cup buttermilk
1 package (1/6 ounce) original Ranch,
  Hidden Valley dressing mix

In a large mixing bowl, combine cabbage, carrots and parsley. Fold in seafood. To prepare dressing, mix remaining ingredients in a small container. Add to salad and mix thoroughly. Serve cold as a main dish or side dish with assorted crackers. Makes 6 servings.

Smoked Fish Log

I make this several times a year. It works best with fresh smoked fish because it is slightly dry and keeps the cream cheese log firm for slicing.

2 cups flaked, smoked fish
1 package (8 ounces) cream cheese,
  softened
1 tablespoon fresh lemon juice
2 teaspoons grated onion
2 teaspoons horseradish

1 teaspoon liquid smoke (if not
  using smoked fish)
1/4 teaspoon salt
1/2 cup chopped pecans
2 tablespoons chopped fresh
  parsley

Combine cheese, lemon juice, onion, horseradish, liquid smoke and salt. Stir in fish and mix thoroughly. Chill mixture for several hours. Combine pecans and parsley. Shape fish mixture into log shape, and roll in nut mixture. Serve with assorted crackers. Makes approximately 8 servings. (*Pictured opposite page 25*)

 Home smoked fish is not shelf stable. Keep it refrigerated.

Florentine Fillets

A colorful fish dish with vegetables rich in vitamin A and C.

1 1/2 pounds skinless, lean fillets
1 can (4 ounces) chopped mushrooms
1 tablespoon canola oil
1/2 cup chopped onion
1 cup crushed saltines
1/4 teaspoon pepper

1/8 teaspoon sage leaves
1 package (10 ounces) frozen
   chopped spinach, thawed
4 teaspoons lemon juice
4 medium tomatoes
Italian dressing

Cut fish into serving-size portions, and set aside. In a small bowl, combine all ingredients except tomatoes and dressing. Arrange fish portions on a prepared baking sheet. Place a spoonful of mushroom mixture on each fillet and top with a tomato slice. Splash with Italian dressing and bake at 350 degrees for 15 minutes. Fish is done when solid white, but still moist. Makes 6 servings.

Fillets with Black Bean-Tomato-Corn Sauce

The southwestern flair has influenced the way we eat for several years. This fillet dish is teamed with popular black beans and other ingredients for a colorful and tasty entree.

1 1/2 pounds fresh fish fillets
4 tablespoons canola oil
1 tablespoon minced fresh ginger or
1 1/2 teaspoons powdered ginger
1 1/3 cups diced fresh tomatoes
1 teaspoon chopped fresh chile
   pepper

1 can (10 ounces) black beans,
   drained
1/2 cup fresh, frozen or canned corn
   kernels
Sour cream or plain yogurt
2 tablespoons chopped fresh
   coriander or cilantro

Cut the fillets into serving-size portions. Lightly salt and pepper each side and saute in 2 tablespoons of oil on each side until fish is done, about 5 to 7 minutes.Meanwhile,combine remaining ingredients except sour cream and coriander in a small saucepan and cook until tomatoes have softened. Place fish on a serving platter and pour sauce over fish. Top each portion with a dollop of sour cream and sprinkle with coriander.Serve with warm tortillas. Makes 6 servings.

Sauteed Fish with Spinach and Bell Pepper Sauce

A colorful and light fillet dish for one of your weekly heart-healthy meals.

1 1/2 pounds skinless fish fillets
3 tablespoons canola oil
2 large red or green bell peppers,
   roasted and peeled
1/2 cup dry white wine
6 tablespoons white wine vinegar

4 fresh thyme sprigs
Salt and pepper
1/2 cup margarine
1 pound cooked fresh spinach
2 tablespoons canola oil

Cut fish into serving-size portions. Halve peppers and puree in processor. In heavy saucepan, boil wine, vinegar and thyme until reduced to 3 tablespoons. Add pepper puree, salt and pepper. Remove from heat and whisk in 2 tablespoons margarine. Over low heat, whisk in remaining margarine. Keep sauce warm on rack over hot water.

Stuffed Fillets with Egg Sauce

Fresh fillets layered with a sumptuous stuffing and topped with the smoothness of a creamy egg sauce. Use a non-oily fish.

2 pounds skinless fish fillets
4 cups fresh bread crumbs
1/2 cup melted margarine
1/4 cup milk
1/4 cup finely chopped onion
2 teaspoons dill weed
2 teaspoons chopped parsley

1 teaspoon thyme
2 eggs, beaten
1/2 teaspoon salt
Dash pepper
2 tablespoons melted margarine
Egg Sauce
Sliced egg for garnish

Rinse fillets and pat dry. Sprinkle with salt and pepper. Place half the fillets in a well-greased baking dish. In large mixing bowl, combine bread crumbs, 1/2 cup melted margarine, milk, onion, dill weed, parsley, thyme, beaten eggs, salt and pepper. Spread stuffing on top of fillets in baking dish. Place remaining fillets on top of stuffing. Baste with 2 tablespoons melted margarine. Bake at 350 degrees for 30 to 35 minutes or until fish is opaque. Cover fish with egg sauce. Makes 4 to 6 servings. To make **EGG SAUCE** melt 1/4 cup margarine in a small saucepan over low heat. Blend in 1/4 cup flour. Add 1 teaspoon dry mustard, 1/2 teaspoon salt and 1/8 teaspoon white pepper. Gradually whisk in 2 cups half-and-half cream. Cook until thick, but do not boil. Stir in 1/4 teaspoon liquid hot pepper sauce, 3 coarsely grated, hard-cooked eggs and 2 tablespoons chopped parsley. Pour sauce over fish. Garnish with egg slices.

Grilled Fish

Consider grilling fish your challenge for the week. The flavor of fish cooked on the outdoor grill is unlike anything you can achieve in the kitchen.

Select fish steaks or fillets at least 3/4 inch thick. To prepare fish for grilling, cut into generous serving-size portions. Rinse and pat dry. Squeeze fresh lemon juice on fish and sprinkle with coarse ground, black pepper and garlic powder if desired. Grill at moderate heat until fish becomes firm and is solid white throughout. Turn once during cooking. Do not overcook. Fish should retain some natural juice.

Asparagus-Stuffed Flounder

When asparagus is in season, try this attractive and delicious way to serve thin fillets. Fish and vegetables make a great team. This idea is from Jane Brody in her **Good Food Book**.

4 to 6 four-ounce fillets
1/2 cup chopped onion
1 1/2 tablespoons margarine
18 young asparagus spears
1 tablespoon flour

1 cup skim milk
1/2 cup grated sharp cheese
Salt and pepper to taste
Dash cayenne and nutmeg

In a small skillet, saute onion in half the margarine for 1 minute. Steam the asparagus until tender-crisp. Rinse fillets and pat dry. Lay the fillets flat and sprinkle the onion evenly over them. Position 3 asparagus spears across each fillet and roll the fillet around them. Secure with a wooden pick. Place in a greased baking dish. In a small saucepan, melt remaining margarine and stir in flour. Cook for 1 minute, then gradually add milk. Cook and stir to make a smooth white sauce. Stir in cheese, salt and peppers. Pour sauce over the fish and sprinkle them with nutmeg. Bake at 350 degrees for 20 minutes. Makes 4 to 6 servings.

Add lots of chopped parsley and a little bit of garlic and tarragon to your favorite mustard, and spread on cold or hot grilled fish.

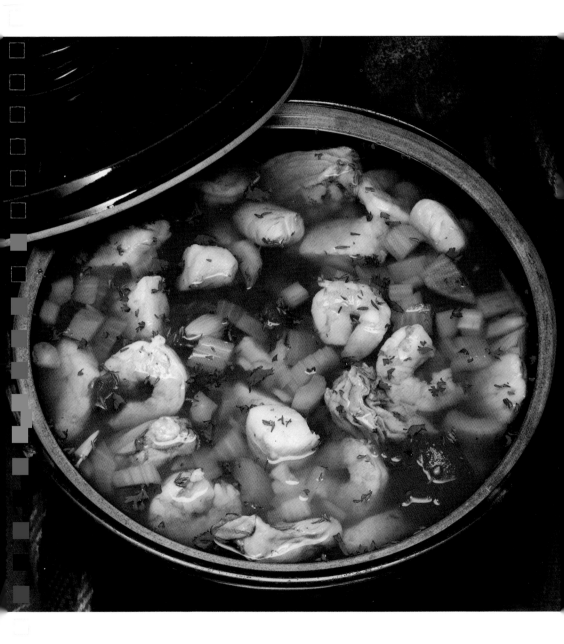

Creole Bouillabaisse, page 46

Smoked Fish Log, page 21

Fillets in Tarragon

A health-conscious fillet dish for a quick, wholesome meal.

1 1/2 pounds fish fillets
1/2 cup plain low fat yogurt
1 tablespoon mayonnaise

1 teaspoon dried tarragon
3/4 cup part-skim mozzarella
   cheese, grated

Cut fish into serving-size portions and place in a baking dish. Mix all other ingredients together and spread over fish. Bake at 350 degrees for 10 minutes or until fish flakes when tested and is opaque. Makes 4 servings.

Fillets with Oriental Sauce

An oily fish with intense flavor works well with this recipe. It's good served with Chinese noodles.

2 pounds skinless fish fillets
1/4 cup orange juice
2 tablespoons canola oil
2 tablespoons soy sauce

1 clove minced garlic
1/8 teaspoon pepper
1 tablespoon fresh lemon juice

Cut fish into serving-size portions and place in a baking dish. Combine remaining ingredients and pour over fish. Bake at 350 for 10 minutes or microwave according to oven directions. Fish is done when it flakes and is opaque. Makes 6 servings.

 Save time when filleting fish by not gutting or scaling it. Just be careful not to slice into the gut area.

Shrimp Butter

This has become a special expected treat for spreading on crackers or hot bread. Add more garlic if you like.

1/2 pound cooked and shredded shrimp
1/4 cup stick-type margarine
1 package (3 ounces) cream cheese

2 cloves minced garlic
1 tablespoon fresh lemon juice
1 tablespoon chopped fresh parsley
1 tablespoon dry sherry

Combine all ingredients by hand or in a food processor. Use as a topping for baked, broiled or grilled fish or spread on crackers or hot bread. Makes 1 cup butter. (Pictured opposite page 61)

Seafood Salad Sandwich

Any freshly flaked or leftover fish combined with olives, onion and celery makes great salads and sandwiches. You could just use your favorite canned tuna salad recipe - try it with fresh fish.

1 1/2 pounds cooked and flaked fish
1/2 cup each chopped stuffed green olives, celery and onions
1/4 cup chopped dill pickle

2/3 cup "lite" mayonnaise
1 1/2 tablespoons horseradish
1 teaspoon pepper
1/4 teaspoon salt

In a large mixing bowl, combine all ingredients well and chill. Serve as a sandwich, salad or chunky dip. Makes 4 to 6 servings.

Label packaged seafoods for the freezer with type of seafood, amount and date.

Seafood Salad Sandwich, page 26

Seafood Sandwich Spread

A fish spread that makes a great lunch at a picnic site, poolside or at home.

2 cups cooked and flaked fish
3 tablespoons drained capers
1/4 cup mayonnaise
1 1/2 tablespoons fresh lemon juice
1/2 cup sliced black olives

2 packages (1/2 ounce each)
   watercress or fresh arugula
2 sliced tomatoes
Sliced red onion
French or Italian bread loaf

Combine all salad ingredients in a mixing bowl. Cut bread into sandwich size portions. Halve each piece lengthwise. Spread fish salad onto each bottom piece. Top with tomato and onion slices, then with top pieces of bread. Serve with a green bean vinaigrette and chips. Makes 4 generous sandwiches.

Fish and 'Kraut Sandwiches

Some like this fish reuben served with a cold, dark beer. For a snack item, use the mini rye round bread.

1 cup cooked, flaked fish
1/2 cup well drained sauerkraut
1/4 cup chopped dill pickles
1/4 cup mayonnaise
1 tablespoon horseradish

12 slices party rye bread
4 slices (1 ounce each) Swiss
   cheese
2 tablespoons margarine

Cook fish by baking, broiling or poaching. Cool and flake. In mixing bowl, combine fish, sauerkraut, pickles, mayonnaise and horseradish. Mix well. Portion mixture evenly on half the bread. Top with cheese. Top with remaining bread. Melt margarine in skillet. Place sandwiches in skillet and grill on each side until golden brown. Serve with chips or relishes and a cold drink. Makes 4 servings.

Sunshine Fillets

A colorful, low calorie preparation with zip and eye appeal. Use any mild flavored fish.

2 pounds skinless fish fillets
3 tablespoons canola oil
2 tablespoons frozen orange juice
   concentrate
2 teaspoons grated fresh orange
   rind

1/2 teaspoon salt
Dash pepper
Dash nutmeg

Cut fillets into serving-size portions. Place portions in a single layer, skin side down, in a prepared baking dish. Combine remaining ingredients and pour over fish. Bake at 350 degrees, for 10 minutes per inch of fish thickness. Makes 4 to 6 servings.

Onion Baked Fillets

Several of my church friends claim this is their favorite of all my recipes. It has a surprise flavor and nice texture.

2 pounds skinless fish fillets
1/2 teaspoon salt
1 cup plain yogurt
1 cup "lite" mayonnaise

1 package (1.6 ounces) original
   ranch salad dressing mix
1 can (2.8 ounces) french fried
   onions, crushed

Cut fillets into serving-size portions. Sprinkle with salt. Combine yogurt, mayonnaise and salad dressing mix in a flat pan. Place crushed onions in another flat pan. Dip fish into yogurt mixture, then press into crushed onions. Place fish on a well-greased baking pan. Bake at 350 degrees for 10 minutes per inch of fish thickness or until fish is opaque. Makes 4 to 6 servings. (Pictured opposite page 42)

Choose your fish, as you do your friends. Look for clear eyes, healthy skin color and no strong body odors.

Crisp Baked Fish

An unusual but tasty topping for crisp fish is found in this unique and tangy variation for baked fillets. Do not use an oily fish for this one.

2 pounds skinless fish fillets
1/4 cup milk
1/4 teaspoon salt

1 cup finely crushed cornflakes, bread or cracker crumbs
2 tablespoons melted margarine
Lemon Lime Relish

Cut fish into serving-size portions. In a flat pan, combine milk and salt. In another pan, place crushed cornflakes or crumbs. Dip fish portions in milk, then in cornflakes. Place on prepared baking sheet. Drizzle fish with margarine. Bake at 350 degrees for 10 minutes per inch of fish thickness. Serve with Lemon Lime Relish. To make **LEMON LIME RELISH**, combine either 1/2 cup sour cream, "lite" mayonnaise or plain yogurt or a combination of the two, 1/4 cup crushed and well drained pineapple, 2 tablespoons diced lemon and lime, 2 tablespoons chopped green pepper, 1 tablespoon minced onion, 1 1/2 tablespoons grated lemon or lime peel, 1/4 teaspoon dry mustard and 1/4 teaspoon celery salt. Makes 1 cup for 4 to 5 servings of fish.

German-Style Baked Fillets

My German father-in-law thought this was great. Fish and sauerkraut offer a simple preparation with a Bavarian influence for any fresh catch.

1 1/2 pounds skinless fish fillets
1/2 cup chopped onion
2 tablespoons margarine or oil
1 can (1 pound, 11 ounces) sauerkraut, drained
1/2 teaspoon caraway seeds

1/2 teaspoon garlic salt
1 package (3 ounces) cream cheese, cubed
1/2 cup grated sharp cheese
1 tablespoon chopped fresh parsley

To cook range-top, cut fish into serving-size portions. Cook onion in margarine in frying pan until tender. Add sauerkraut, 1/2 cup water, caraway seeds and garlic salt. Cover and simmer for 10 minutes or until flavors are well blended. Top with fish pieces. Arrange cream cheese cubes about the mixture. Cover and simmer for seven minutes or until fish is opaque throughout. Sprinkle with grated cheese. Allow cheese to melt and sprinkle with parsley. To bake in the oven, prepare in a casserole dish and bake at 350 degrees for 10 minutes per inch of fish thickness. Serve with dark rye bread and a crisp salad. Makes four servings.

Savory Baked Fillets

The two popular flavors of bacon and onion turn economical fillets into an elegant, yet low calorie entree. Use any fish.

2 pounds skinless fish fillets
2 teaspoons lemon juice
1/4 teaspoon pepper
6 slices lean bacon

1 medium, thinly sliced onion
1/2 cup soft bread crumbs
2 tablespoons chopped fresh
  parsley

Place fillets in a single layer in a prepared baking dish. Sprinkle with lemon juice and pepper. Fry bacon until crisp, drain and crumble. Cook onion rings in bacon grease until tender then arrange evenly over fillets. Combine bacon, bread crumbs, and parsley. Sprinkle mixture over fillets and onion. Bake at 350 degrees for 10 minutes per inch of fish thickness or until fillets are opaque throughout. Makes 4 to 6 servings.

Fillets Veronique

In the romantic tradition of classic French cuisine, lean fish fillets are gently poached in white wine and served with a natural sauce. Serve this one for an unhurried, relaxing dinner.

2 pounds fresh fish fillets
2 tablespoons lemon juice
2 teaspoons salt
1 cup dry white wine
1 cup (1/4 pound) green seedless
  grapes

1/4 teaspoon fines herbs
3 tablespoons margarine or butter
2 tablespoons flour

Sprinkle fillets with lemon juice and salt and arrange in a well-greased skillet in one or two layers. Combine wine, grapes and fines herbs. Pour mixture over fish and heat to simmering. Cover and poach for 5 minutes or until fish flakes. Carefully transfer fish to oven-proof platter. Reserve liquid and grapes. In a small saucepan over medium heat, melt margarine and blend in flour. Add reserved liquid gradually and cook until smooth, but not thick, stirring constantly. Pour sauce over fish and garnish with reserved grapes. Fish may be heated under the broiler until lightly browned. Makes 4 to 6 servings.

Fillets Tomatillo

This is our adaptation of the recipe that took Brian Coates, executive chef of the Ice House Restaurant in Fort Worth, to the final cookoff in the first Texas Seafood Challenge.

2 pounds skinless fish fillets
2 tablespoons olive oil
2 cups chopped tomatillos or tomatoes
1/2 cup each chopped onion and celery
1/4 cup chopped bell pepper
2 cloves chopped garlic
1 can (4 ounces) green chilies

1/2 teaspoon oregano
1/2 cup clam juice or fish stock
1 teaspoon chopped fresh celantro or parsley
Juice from 1 lime
1/4 teaspoon white pepper
1/4 teaspoon cayenne pepper
1 teaspoon cumin
Salt to taste

In a saucepan, saute tomatillos, onion, celery, bell pepper and garlic in olive oil for 5 minutes. Cool mixture slightly and coarsely chop in blender or food processor. Return to saucepan and add all other ingredients except fish. Simmer for 15 minutes to reduce liquid. Bake fillets at 350 degrees for 10 minutes per inch of fish thickness. Place fish on heated platter and spoon sauce over top. Garnish with a tomato skin rose or as desired. This sauce is also delicious with broiled, grilled or pan fried fish and shrimp. Makes 4 servings.

Fillets in Nut Crust

A simplified version that took my friend, Master Chef Victor Gielisse of Actuelle in Dallas to the American Seafood Challenge after twice being named Texas' Best Seafood Chef. Look for his book, **Cuisine Actuelle**.

2 pounds skinless fish fillets of snapper, pompano, drum or other firm, lean fish
1/3 cup flour
1 cup fresh whole wheat bread crumbs

1 cup finely chopped pecans
1 egg yolk and 2 egg whites
2 tablespoons olive or canola oil

Cut fish into serving-size portions. Lightly dust with flour. Combine crumbs and nuts in a flat pan. Beat egg yolk and whites with 2 tablespoons water in another pan. Dredge each fish portion in egg wash, then in crumb-nut mixture. Carefully place fish on a baking sheet and drizzle with oil. Bake for 10 minutes per inch of thickness at 350 degrees. Makes 5 to 6 servings. (Pictured opposite page 32)

Fillets and Wild Rice Anne Marie

These mild flavored baked fillets, named after my Mom, are topped with savory wild rice and balanced with a chunky, mushroom-walnut sauce. It's company food and tastes very special.

2 pounds fresh fish fillets
1 teaspoon salt
1/4 teaspoon pepper
3 slices chopped bacon
1 cup chopped fresh mushrooms
1/4 cup minced onion

1/4 cup minced celery
2 cups cooked wild rice
1/2 teaspoon salt
2 tablespoons melted margarine
Mushroom-Walnut Sauce

Cut fillets into serving-size portions and season with salt and pepper. In a skillet, cook bacon until lightly browned. Add mushrooms, onion and celery, and cook until tender. Stir in cooked rice and salt. Place fish in a well-prepared baking pan. Spoon rice mixture on top of fish portions. Drizzle melted margarine over rice. Cover and bake at 350 degrees for about 20 minutes or until fish flakes and is opaque. Serve with Mushroom-Walnut Sauce. Makes 6 servings. To make **MUSHROOM-WALNUT SAUCE**, melt 3 tablespoons margarine in a saucepan. Add 1 tablespoon minced onion and 1 cup sliced mushrooms. Cook until tender. Stir in 3 tablespoons flour, 1/2 teaspoon dry mustard, 1/2 teaspoon salt and 1/4 teaspoon thyme. Gradually stir in 2 cups half-and-half cream. Cook over medium heat until thickened, stirring constantly. Stir in 1/4 cup toasted walnuts. Serve sauce over fish and wild rice. Makes approximately 2-1/2 cups sauce.

Baked Fillets Cheesy

Shredded Swiss cheese and tomatoes provide color and unique flavor to any available fish fillets.

2 pounds skinless fillets
2 tablespoons grated onion
1/2 teaspoon salt
1/8 teaspoon pepper

2 large chopped tomatoes
1/4 cup melted margarine
1 cup shredded Swiss cheese

Place fillets in a single layer on a well-greased bake-and-serve platter. Sprinkle with onion, salt and pepper, and cover with tomato pieces. Drizzle margarine over fillets and bake for 10 to 12 minutes at 350 degrees, or until fish is opaque. Sprinkle fish with cheese and broil 2 to 3 minutes longer, or until cheese melts. Makes 4 to 6 servings.

Fillets in Nut Crust, page 31

Broiled Fillets Mexicali

A simple and spicy flair to broiled fillets. Serve it with your favorite Mexican side dish.

2 pounds skinless fish fillets
1 can (4 ounces) chopped green
  chilies
2 tablespoons canola oil
2 tablespoons soy sauce
2 tablespoons Worcestershire
  sauce

2 teaspoons paprika
1/2 teaspoon chili powder
1/2 teaspoon garlic powder
Dash liquid hot pepper sauce

Cut fillets into serving-size portions and place in a single layer on a prepared baking dish. Combine remaining ingredients and pour sauce over fillets. Broil approximately 4 inches from source of heat for 5 minutes or until fish is opaque. Baste once with natural juices during broiling. Makes 4 to 6 servings.

Blackened Fillets

This is our most popular recipe for that spicy, cajun preparation made famous by Paul Prudhomme. My change for a more healthy approach is to bake the fish. Use a firm texture fish.

2 pounds skinless firm fish fillets
1/4 cup melted margarine
1 tablespoon paprika
1 teaspoon salt
1 teaspoon onion powder
1 teaspoon garlic powder

3/4 teaspoon black pepper
3/4 teaspoon white pepper
1/2 teaspoon cayenne pepper
1/2 teaspoon dried thyme leaves
1/2 teaspoon dried oregano leaves

Cut the fish into serving-size portions. Place margarine in a flat pan. Dip both sides of fish in margarine. Combine dry ingredients in a flat pan. Dredge both sides of the fish into the mixture, pressing the spices in with your fingers. Place the fish on a baking pan. Bake for 10 minutes per inch of fish thickness or grill just until fish is solid white and flakes. Makes 4 to 6 servings.

Fillets Amandine

A classic — an easy and elegant fillet dish with broiled lemon and buttery almonds.

2 pounds skinless, small fish fillets
1/4 cup flour
1/2 teaspoon seasoned salt
1 teaspoon paprika

1/4 cup melted margarine
1/2 cup sliced almonds
Juice of 1 lemon
1 tablespoon chopped fresh parsley

Cut fillets into serving-size portions if large. Combine flour, seasoned salt and paprika. Roll fish in flour mixture and place in a single layer in a prepared baking dish. Drizzle 2 tablespoons melted margarine over fish. Broil about 4 inches from source of heat for 5 to 6 minutes or until fish is opaque. While fish is broiling, saute almonds in remaining margarine until golden brown, stirring constantly. Remove from heat and mix in lemon juice and parsley. Spoon almond mixture over fish and serve at once. Makes 4 to 6 servings.

Sailor's Fish Boil

A hearty and diverse combination of Texas fish and produce topped with a sassy sauce. And it's easy to increase for a crowd. Use thick, firm fish.

2 pounds skinless fish fillets or
  steaks
12 small red potatoes
6 medium peeled onions
1 head green cabbage, cut into
  wedges

1 can (1 pound) small whole beets
Chopped fresh parsley
Horseradish Sauce

Cut fish into serving-size portions or chunks. Bring a large pot of salted water to a boil. Remove a 1/2-inch strip of peeling from around the middle of each potato. Add potatoes and onions to water. Reduce the heat and simmer for 10 minutes or until tender. Add cabbage wedges and simmer for 10 minutes. Add fish and simmer 3 to 4 minutes or until fish is opaque throughout. Remove vegetables and fish to a serving platter and keep warm. Heat beets in remaining water and add to platter. Pour Horseradish Sauce over vegetables and fish. Sprinkle with chopped parsley. Makes 6 servings. To make **HORSERADISH SAUCE**, combine 1/2 cup prepared horserad-ish, 1 tablespoon flour, 1/4 teaspoon paprika and 1/4 teaspoon salt in a small saucepan. Stir in 1 cup half-and-half and cook until thickened, stirring constantly. Makes 1 1/2 cups of sauce.

Christmas Cranberry Catch

This festive Christmas Eve dish is a tradition in our home, and a hearty and tasty way to welcome St. Nick.

2 pounds thick fish fillets
1 cup sliced celery
1/3 cup chopped onions
6 tablespoons margarine
4 cups soft bread cubes (1/2-inch)

1/2 cup chopped pecans
3/4 teaspoon salt
1 teaspoon grated orange rind
1/4 cup orange juice
Cranberry Orange Sauce

Cut fillets into six portions. Rinse and pat dry. In a fry pan, cook celery and onions in 4 tablespoons margarine until tender but not brown. Stir in bread cubes, pecans, 1/4 teaspoon salt, orange rind and orange juice. Turn stuffing into well-greased baking dish. Arrange fish in a single layer on stuffing. Drizzle remaining two tablespoons melted margarine over fish. Sprinkle with 1/2 teaspoon salt. Bake at 350 degrees for 10 minutes per inch of fish thickness or until fish is opaque throughout. Top with Cranberry Orange Sauce. Makes 6 servings. To make **CRANBERRY ORANGE SAUCE** combine 1/2 cup sugar and 2 teaspoons cornstarch in a two-quart saucepan. Add 1/2 cup orange juice and 1/2 cup water. Cook and stir constantly, until mixture comes to a boil. Add 1 cup raw cranberries and cook for 5 minutes, stirring occasionally, until skins on cranberries pop. Fold in 2 teaspoons orange rind. Serve over fish. Makes 1 1/4 cups sauce.

Picante Fillets

I've cooked hundreds of batches of this for taste-testers in grocery stores. Responses are always the same. "Is that all there is to it?" It's hot, it's good. It's Texan! So simple, it's perfect for a fast meal for adult tastes.

1 1/2 pounds fish fillets
1 jar (1 lb. 8 ounces) mild or medium
   picante sauce

2 tablespoons canola oil
2 cups hot, cooked rice

Cut fish into serving-size portions. Rinse and pat dry. Heat oil in skillet and sear fish on both sides. Add the picante sauce and simmer fish for 5 to 7 minutes. Serve over hot rice. Makes 6 servings.

 When baking or broiling fillets, turn under the thin end of the fillet to make it more even in thickness.

Fish in Orange Horseradish Cashew Crust

Inspired by talented Chef Alex Breslin formerly of Dallas, this recipe teams together the unique flavors of horseradish, nuts and orange to complement the fish. The chef suggests snapper or grouper.

1 1/2 pounds fish fillets
1 egg white
1 tablespoon horseradish
1/2 cup cornbread crumbs

1/4 cup cashew nuts, blended or chopped in food processor
1 tablespoon grated fresh orange rind

Cut fish into serving-size portions. Rinse and pat dry. In a flat pan, whisk egg white, horseradish and 2 tablespoons water together. In another pan, combine cornbread crumbs, nuts and orange rind. Dip fish in egg white mixture, then press nut mixture into fish. Place on prepared baking pan and bake at 350 degrees for ten minutes per inch of thickness. Makes 6 servings.

Fillets Wellington

A delicious fillet dish with richly seasoned crab stuffing, encased in a crisp, buttery fish-shaped crust. What a fun presentation!

2 large fillets (1/2 pound each) or 1 pound of small fillets
1 tablespoon lemon juice
1/4 teaspoon salt
1/4 teaspoon pepper

Crab stuffing
1 can (8 ounces) refrigerated crescent rolls
1 egg yolk

Season fillets with lemon juice, then salt and pepper. Set aside. To make crab stuffing, combine 1/2 pound flaked crab meat, 1 egg white, 1/3 cup whipping cream, 1/2 cup chopped celery, 1/2 cup bread crumbs, 1/4 cup melted margarine and 1 teaspoon lemon pepper. Separate the roll dough into two portions. On a lightly floured board, roll out half the dough and cut into a fish shape. Cut the second fish shape 1 inch bigger, all the way around. Place the first shape on a greased baking sheet and spread a thin layer of crab stuffing on it. Lay a fillet on the dough and spread half of the crab mixture on top. Layer with remaining fillet and cover top and sides with remaining stuffing. Place second fish shaped dough on top and pinch edges together to seal. Use scrap dough to make fins, eyes and gill slits. Brush with egg yolk and water mixture. Bake for 10 minutes at 425 degrees then for 15 minutes at 350 degrees or until crust is brown. Makes 4 servings.

Sweet and Sour Fish

Pineapple, water chestnuts, green pepper, soy sauce, and brown sugar combine with firm, thick fillets to capture the culinary charm of the south sea. This is also wonderful with shrimp or scallops.

2 pounds fish fillets
3 tablespoons cooking oil
1 can (1 lb. 4 oz.) pineapple chunks
1 1/4 cups liquid (pineapple syrup and water)
1/4 cup cider vinegar
1/4 cup brown sugar, packed
3 tablespoons cornstarch
1 tablespoon soy sauce

1/2 teaspoon salt
1/2 teaspoon garlic salt
1 can (6 oz.) water chestnuts, drained and sliced
1 medium green pepper, cut into 1 inch squares
1 medium tomato, cut into thin wedges
1 1/2 cups cooked rice

Cut fillets into 1 inch pieces. Drain pineapple chunks, reserving syrup. Add water to syrup to measure 1 1/4 cups liquid. In a small bowl, combine liquid, vinegar, brown sugar, cornstarch, soy sauce and salts, and blend well. In a large skillet, saute fish in oil for 5 minutes. Add liquid mixture to fish and cook, stirring gently, for about 2 minutes or until sauce is thick and clear. Add remaining ingredients and cook until vegetables are tender-crisp and fish is opaque throughout. Serve over hot rice. Makes 4 to 6 servings.

Just Right Fried Fish

Bill Berkley of Rockport has perfected fried fish that pleases friends and family alike.

2 pounds fish fillets, any kind
2 cups milk
1 egg
1 tablespoon Dijon mustard
1 tablespoon liquid hot pepper sauce

2 cups yellow cornmeal
1 teaspoon white pepper
1 tablespoon seasoned salt
1 teaspoon garlic powder
Canola oil for frying

Cut fish into serving-size portions, large chunks or fingers. Rinse, drain and set aside. In a flat pan, mix together milk, egg, mustard and hot pepper sauce. In another pan, mix cornmeal and seasonings together. Dip fish in batter and then in cornmeal mixture, coating well. Shake off excess. Fry in hot oil at 365 degrees until crisp and golden. Drain and serve with a seafood sauce if desired. Makes 4 hearty servings.

Buttermilk Fried Fillets

If you **must** fry and like a heavy batter, try this. The trick is fresh fish and hot oil.

2 pounds skinless fish fillets
1 cup buttermilk
1 cup biscuit mix

2 teaspoons salt
Canola oil for frying

Cut fillets into serving-size portions. Place portions in a single layer in a shallow dish. Pour buttermilk over portions and let stand for 30 minutes, turning once. Combine biscuit mix and salt. Remove portions from buttermilk and roll in biscuit mix. Deep fry in hot oil for 4 to 5 minutes or until brown. Turn carefully and fry 4 to 5 minutes longer or until fish is brown and flakes easily when tested with a fork. Drain on absorbent paper. Serve with lemon wedges or malt vinegar. Makes 4 to 6 servings.

Spicy Pan Fried Fish

A spicy way to tolerate the hassle of small pan-fish. I use croaker.

3 pounds pan-dressed fish
1 cup yellow cornmeal
1 teaspoon salt
1/2 teaspoon pepper
1 1/2 teaspoons paprika

1/2 teaspoon celery salt
1/4 teaspoon dry mustard
1/4 teaspoon onion powder
Canola oil for frying
Lemon wedges

Clean, wash and dry fish. Combine dry ingredients then roll fish in the mixture. Fry fish in shallow oil in a large fry pan over moderate heat for 4 to 5 minutes. Turn carefully and fry 4 to 5 minutes longer, or until fish flakes easily when tested with a fork. Drain on absorbent paper and serve with lemon wedges. Makes 6 to 8 servings.

Place fillets or dressed fish on top of lemon slices to bake or broil. This adds flavor and keeps the fish from sticking to the pan.

Stuffed Flounder

A popular preparation for this flat fish. Prepare with crab meat, shrimp or cheese stuffing for an impressive entree.

4 small whole flounder
1 cup flaked crab meat
1/4 cup margarine
3 tablespoons each chopped onion, celery and bell pepper
1 clove minced garlic
1 cup crushed cracker crumbs

2 tablespoons chopped fresh parsley
1 teaspoon dry mustard
1/4 cup chicken broth
1 beaten egg
1 teaspoon Worcestershire sauce

Clean and scale the flounder. Remove the heads if desired and wash the fish. Make an incision down the middle on the top side of the fish. With the knife parallel to the fish, cut the flesh away from the backbone on each side to make a "pocket" for the stuffing. Do not cut through the fin area. Saute vegetables in margarine. Combine vegetables and all other ingredients in mixing bowl. Loosely stuff flounder with mixture. Sprinkle with paprika. Wrap tail in aluminum foil. Baste fish with cooking oil or margarine. Bake for 10 minutes per inch of thickness at 350 degrees, basting once. Fish is done when the flesh flakes and is solid white. Makes 4 servings.

Fillets with Cumin-Garlic Butter

For garlic lovers! This fish dish is simple and tasty and easy on the budget.

1 1/2 pounds skinless, lean fish fillets
2 tablespoons canola oil
2 tablespoons fresh lemon juice
2 teaspoons ground cumin
1 teaspoon minced garlic
Salt and freshly ground pepper to taste

1/2 cup margarine or unsalted butter
2 tablespoon minced garlic
2 teaspoons ground cumin
1 1/2 teaspoons paprika
1 teaspoon fresh lemon juice

Cut fish into serving-size portions and place in a shallow baking dish. Combine oil, lemon juice, cumin, garlic, salt and pepper. Pour marinade over fish rubbing the mixture on both sides of the fillets. Place in the refrigerator for 1 hour. Meanwhile, combine remaining ingredients in small bowl to make cumin-garlic butter. After fish has marinated, spread seasoned butter on top of each fillet. Broil fish about 4 inches from heat source for 5 to 7 minutes. Fish is done when solid white, but still juicy. Makes 4 generous servings.

Lemon Fillets with Thyme

Fresh fillets seasoned and enveloped in a lemon-thyme broth and served on hot rice.

2 pounds skinless fish fillets
1/4 cup flour
1/2 teaspoon salt
1/4 teaspoon pepper
2 tablespoons olive oil
1/2 cup chopped onions
1 tablespoon margarine

1 cup chicken broth
3 tablespoons lemon juice
1/2 teaspoon thyme
2 tablespoons chopped fresh
  parsley
3 cups hot cooked rice

Rinse fish and cut into serving-size portions. In a flat pan, combine flour, salt and pepper. Dredge fish in mixture. In a large skillet, heat oil and sear fish for 1 to 2 minutes on each side. Transfer fish to serving platter. Add onion and margarine to skillet and cook until onion is soft. Stir in remaining flour mixture, broth, 2 tablespoons lemon juice and thyme. Cook and stir until smooth, about 1 minute. Return fish to skillet, reduce heat, cover and cook until fish flakes and is opaque throughout, about 4 minutes. Place hot rice on serving platter. Arrange fish on top of rice. Stir remaining lemon juice into sauce and pour over fish. Sprinkle with parsley. Serve with additional lemon wedges and steamed broccoli as a flavor contrast. Makes 4 to 6 servings.

Light Seafood Casserole

A heart-healthy fish entree that is attractive, tasty and easy to prepare.

2 cups cooked and flaked fish or
  crab meat
1 cup toasted whole wheat bread
  cubes
1 cup chopped celery
1/2 cup chopped red or green bell
  pepper

1/2 chopped onion
1 cup low fat cottage cheese
1/2 cup part skim grated mozzarella
  cheese
2 tablespoons "lite" mayonnaise
2 tablespoons fresh lemon juice
1 teaspoon Worcestershire sauce

In a large mixing bowl, combine fish, toast cubes, vegetables and cheeses. In a small container, mix together mayonnaise, lemon juice and Worcestershire sauce. Fold into fish mixture and place into baking dish. Bake at 350 degrees for 20 minutes or until casserole is hot and cheese is melted. Makes 4 servings.

Broiled Fish With Herb Sauce

So simple and quick—just right when time is short. The only trick is to use good quality fish.

1 pound fish steaks or fillets
1 tablespoon margarine
1/4 cup dry white wine

1 tablespoon chopped fresh parsley
1/4 teaspoon fine herbs
1 clove, minced garlic

In a saucepan, combine margarine, wine, parsley, herbs and garlic. Heat slowly until margarine is melted. Place fish on broiler pan and brush fish with sauce. Broil 4 inches from heat source for 5 minutes. Turn carefully, brush with sauce and broil 2 minutes longer. Fish is done when solid white and flakes, but is still juicy. Makes 4 servings.

Pan Seared Fish On Curried Roasted Vegetables

The philosophy of Master Chef Victor Gielisse of Dallas is to stick to the basics and use fresh, wholesome ingredients. This is an example of his teachings using snapper or other moderately lean fish.

2 pounds skinless fish fillets
Salt and pepper to taste
6 tablespoons olive or canola oil
Flour for dusting
1 minced red onion
3 cloves minced garlic

1 1/2 teaspoons curry powder
1/2 cup each julienne cut jicama,
**   carrots, leeks and celery**
2 tablespoons teriyaki or soy sauce
2 tablespoons chopped cilantro

Cut fillets into serving-size portions. Season fish with salt and pepper. Dust with flour and saute in 3 tablespoons oil until lightly browned on both sides. Remove from pan and set aside. Meanwhile, heat remaining oil in a skillet and saute onion and garlic over low heat for 1 minute. Stir in curry powder. Add vegetables and saute over high heat for 1 minute. Place vegetables in a baking dish. Add teriyaki and cilantro and a dash of salt. Top with fish. Bake at 350 degrees for 5 to 7 minutes. Serve immediately. Makes 6 servings.

 Use fresh herbs when available for a more pronounced flavor.

Fish and Potato Roast

This is a Mediterranean dish originating with a fish called pargo, a type of sea bream. I use thick fillets like snapper, grouper or tilefish.

2 pounds thick, skinless fish fillets
3 large russet potatoes
3 thinly sliced garlic cloves
4 tablespoons chopped fresh
  parsley
1 small sliced onion
1 large chopped tomato
1 green bell pepper, cut into rings

1/2 teaspoon dried thyme
Salt and coarse ground pepper to
  taste
4 thin slices lemon
1 tablespoon olive oil
1 bay leaf, broken in half
1/4 cup dry sherry

Cut fish into serving-size portions. Peel, rinse and drain potatoes. Slice and spread half of the potatoes in the bottom of a lightly oiled shallow 3-quart baking dish. Combine garlic, parsley, onions, tomatoes and peppers and arrange on top. Season with thyme, salt, and pepper. Finish with the remaining potatoes. Pour 1 cup of water over the mixture and cover with foil. Bake for 45 minutes at 350 degrees. Meanwhile, season fish with salt and pepper. After the potatoes have baked, raise the oven temperature to 425 degrees. Remove the baking dish from the oven. Nestle the fish, skinned side down into the bed of potatoes and vegetables. Lay the lemon slices on top and drizzle with oil. Tuck the bay leaf under the fish and return the dish, uncovered, to the top oven rack. Bake for about 10 minutes until the fish is opaque and still moist. Spoon sherry over the fish and return to the oven for 2 minutes. Remove the bay leaf. Makes 6 servings.

Batter Fried Shark

Put the bite on shark with this old English favorite. This is good breading for any fish.

2 pounds shark fillets or other fish
1 cup flour
1 1/2 teaspoons salt

1 teaspoon baking powder
1 tablespoon white vinegar
Oil for frying

Cut fillets into 1-inch pieces. Combine flour, salt and baking powder. Slowly add 1 cup water and vinegar. Mix well. Dip fish cubes into batter and drop into hot oil, 365 degrees. Cool 3 to 4 minutes or until golden brown. Drain on absorbent paper. Makes 6 servings.

Onion Baked Fillets, page 28

Fish Turbans Florentine

An eye-catching fillet recipe, rolled to envelop a savory spinach stuffing and topped with a creamy shrimp sauce. Use thin, lean fillets.

4 to 6 skinless fillets, 6 to 8 inches long

1 package (6 1/2 ounces) seasoned bread croutons

1 package (10 ounces) frozen, chopped spinach, well drained

1/8 teaspoon each salt and pepper

1/4 cup melted margarine

1 beaten egg

1/4 teaspoon thyme

1/8 teaspoon pepper

Pimiento for garnish

Shrimp Sauce

Rinse fillets and pat dry. Place fillets, skinned side up, on a clean working surface. Sprinkle with salt and pepper. In a large mixing bowl, combine croutons, spinach and remaining ingredients except pimiento and sauce. Place a portion of stuffing on each fillet. With thin end of fillet on top, skewer ends of fish together with wooden picks. Stand turbans on end in lightly greased baking dish. Bake at 350 degrees for 20 to 25 minutes or until fish is opaque. Extra stuffing can be baked separately or used in another meal. To make **SHRIMP SAUCE**, combine one can (10 1/2 ounces) cream of shrimp soup, 1/2 cup chopped shrimp and 1/4 cup milk. Heat and pour over turbans. Garnish with pimiento strips. Makes 4 to 6 servings.

Light and Crispy Fish

This is as good as it sounds without the calories of deep frying. Any fish will do.

1 pound snapper fillets or other fish

2 tablespoons grated Parmesan cheese

3 tablespoons cornmeal or seasoned bread crumbs

1/2 teaspoon pepper

1/4 teaspoon onion salt

1/2 teaspoon paprika

1 tablespoon soft, diet margarine

Cut fish into serving-size portions or "fingers." Rinse fish and pat dry. Combine cheese, cornmeal and seasonings in a flat pan. Coat fish with the mixture and place the fish on a prepared baking pan. Drizzle margarine over fish. Bake about 10 minutes per inch of fish thickness at 350 degrees, or until solid white throughout. Do not overcook. Makes 4 servings.

Seafood Creole

Seafood, rice and roux are blended and seasoned to capture the essence of Creole cookery.

2 pounds peeled and deveined shrimp or fish fillets cut into 1-inch pieces
2 tablespoons margarine
2 tablespoons flour
1 can (10 ounces) tomatoes, chopped (reserve liquid)
1 can (8 ounces) tomato sauce
1/2 cup each chopped green onions and tops, bell pepper and fresh parsley

2 whole bay leaves
4 cloves chopped garlic
1/2 teaspoon salt
1/2 teaspoon thyme
Dash cayenne pepper
1 lemon slice
Hot cooked rice

Prepare roux by melting margarine in large skillet. Over medium heat, blend in flour and stir constantly until roux is dark brown. Be careful not to scorch. In a 1-cup measurer, add reserved tomato liquid and enough water to equal 1 cup. Stir into roux, and blend until smooth. Add remaining ingredients except seafood and rice. Cover and simmer for 10 minutes. Add shrimp or fish and cook for five minutes. Remove bay leaves and serve creole with hot rice. Makes 6 servings.

Heavenly Fillets

This recipe always demands an encore. It really **is** heavenly. Try it with a mild flavored fish.

2 pounds skinless fish fillets
2 tablespoons lemon juice
1/4 cup grated Parmesan cheese
2 tablespoons margarine

2 tablespoons "lite" mayonnaise
3 tablespoons chopped green onion
1/4 teaspoon salt
Dash liquid hot pepper sauce

Cut fish into serving-size portions and place in a single layer on well-greased baking platter. Brush with lemon juice. In a small bowl, combine remaining ingredients. Broil fish 4 inches from source of heat for five minutes or until fish is opaque throughout. Remove from heat and spread with cheese mixture. Broil two more minutes or until lightly browned. Makes 4 to 6 servings.

Cioppino

A variety of fish and shellfish is stewed in a tomato-based broth — a good idea brought to San Francisco by Italian immigrants.

1 1/2 pounds fresh fish fillets
1/2 pound rock shrimp, or regular shrimp, split and cleaned
12 squid, peeled and cleaned
12 hardshell clams or mussels
1/4 cup olive oil
1 medium chopped green pepper
1 medium chopped onion
2 cloves minced garlic

4 ounces fresh mushrooms, or one small can mushroom slices
1 can (1 pound, 12 ounces) stewed tomatoes
2 cans (8 ounces each) tomato sauce
1 1/2 teaspoons seasoned salt
1/4 teaspoon pepper
1 cup dry white wine

Cut fillets and squid into 1-inch cubes. Cook green pepper, onion, garlic, and mushroom slices in olive oil until tender. Add canned tomatoes with liquid, tomato sauce, seasoned salt, pepper and 2 cups water. Bring mixture to a boil, then reduce heat and simmer for 30 minutes, stirring occasionally. Add fish, shrimp, clams and wine. Cover and simmer for 15 minutes, stirring occasionally. Add squid and cook for 2 minutes. Serve in large soup bowls with chunks of hot French bread. Makes 6 servings.

Festive Fillets

Kids like it. It's colorful, crumbly and easy on the cook. Use any fish.

2 pounds skinless fillets
1/2 cup French dressing
1 1/2 cups crushed cheese crackers

2 tablespoons canola oil
Paprika

Cut fillets into serving-size portions. Place dressing in one flat pan and crushed crackers in another. Dip fish in dressing, then press into cracker crumbs on both sides. Place fish in a well-greased baking pan and drizzle with oil. Bake at 350 degrees for 10 minutes per inch of fish thickness, or until fish is opaque. Makes 4 to 6 servings.

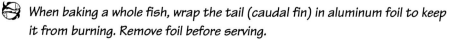 *When baking a whole fish, wrap the tail (caudal fin) in aluminum foil to keep it from burning. Remove foil before serving.*

Seafood Bisque

A hearty combination of shrimp, oysters and crab meat is simmered in a thick broth. This has been around for ages and is a winter favorite.

1/2 pound shrimp, peeled and deveined
1/2 pint fresh oysters
1/2 pound fresh blue crab meat
3 tablespoons minced celery
3 tablespoons chopped green onions and tops
2 tablespoons minced bell pepper
1/2 cup melted margarine or butter

1 can (10 1/2 ounces) condensed cream of shrimp soup
1 can (13 ounces) evaporated milk
1/2 cup milk
1/2 teaspoon salt
1/8 teaspoon pepper
1/2 teaspoon thyme
2 tablespoons dry sherry

Cut large shrimp in half. Remove any remaining shell or cartilage from crab meat. In a large stew pot, cook celery, onions and bell pepper in margarine until tender. Add shrimp, oysters and crab meat. Cook over low heat until shrimp turn pink and oysters curl at the edges. Add remaining ingredients and heat to a near boil. Serve immediately. Makes 4 to 6 servings.

Creole Bouillabaisse

A soup of French Mediterranean origin made by fishermen's wives from unsold portions of their husbands' catches. Recipes have changed, but the principle remains — use an assortment of seafood.

1 pound fresh fish fillets, cut in 1 1/2-inch chunks
1 pint fresh oysters
1 pound fresh shrimp, peeled and deveined
1/4 cup margarine
1/4 cup flour
1 cup chopped onions
1/2 cup chopped celery
2 cloves minced garlic

1/4 cup chopped fresh parsley
2 cans (13 ounces each) chicken broth
1 large can (1 pound, 12 ounces) tomatoes, undrained, cut up
1 bottle (8 ounces) clam juice
1 cup dry white wine
1 tablespoon fresh lemon juice
1 bay leaf
1/4 teaspoon salt
1/4 teaspoon cayenne pepper

Melt margarine in large boiler pot over medium heat. To prepare roux, slowly blend in flour and stir constantly until mixture is light brown. Add onions, celery, garlic and parsley and continue stirring until vegetables are tender. Gradually whisk in chicken broth. Add remaining ingredients except seafood. Bring to a boil, then simmer for 10 minutes. Add fish and oysters and simmer for 5 minutes. Add shrimp and cook for 5 minutes more or until all seafood is done. Makes 8 servings. (Pictured opposite page 24)

Shrimp Puppies

Hush puppies never had it so good. Try this streamlined version with shrimp.

2 cups cooked and shredded Texas
   shrimp
2 packages (6 ounces each)
   jalapeño cornbread mix
1 can (1 pound 1 ounce) cream style
   corn

1/4 cup chopped green onions and
   tops
1 finely chopped jalapeño pepper
Oil for frying

Shred cooked shrimp in a food processor or chop finely with a knife. In a large mixing bowl, combine all ingredients. Heat oil to 365 degrees. Drop mixture by heaping teaspoonfuls into hot oil. Deep fry until golden brown. Remove from oil and drain on absorbent paper. Makes 5 dozen puppies. (*Pictured opposite page 49*)

Stuffed Shrimp

A classy way to make shrimp an extra special hors d'oeuvre or entree.

12 large shrimp, at least 10/15
   count
1 1/2 cups fresh bread crumbs
1/4 cup margarine
3 tablespoons minced celery
2 cloves minced garlic

3 tablespoons sherry
1/2 teaspoon dried thyme
1/4 teaspoon each salt and pepper
2 tablespoons chopped fresh
   parsley
Paprika

Butterfly shrimp by removing shell except for last tail segment. On underside of shrimp tails, cut nearly all the way through. Slightly flatten tails by pressing with fingers. Arrange shrimp on a prepared baking sheet. Saute celery and garlic in margarine. In a small mixing bowl, combine all ingredients except shrimp and paprika. Place at least a tablespoon of the stuffing on each shrimp. Sprinkle with paprika and bake for 5 minutes at 350 degrees. Makes six hors d'oeuvre servings or two main dish servings.

Shrimp Egg Rolls

Chopped Texas shrimp and vegetables sauteed Chinese style make great egg rolls.

3/4 pound raw, chopped shrimp
3 tablespoons peanut or canola oil
1 cup shredded cabbage
1/4 pound fresh bean sprouts
1/2 pound fresh green beans, in thin, diagonal slices
1/2 cup shredded carrots

1/4 cup chopped onion
1 clove minced garlic
1/4 teaspoon each, salt and dry mustard
Square egg roll wrappers
Oil for frying

In a skillet, saute shrimp and add each remaining ingredient, except wrappers, every 1 to 2 minutes. Vegetables should remain tender-crisp. Place 1/4 to 1/3 cup mixture on each egg roll wrapper. Fold sides in approximately 1 inch. Roll up and "seal" with a thin paste of cornstarch and water. Deep fry at 365 degrees until golden brown. Drain on absorbent paper. Serve with soy sauce, hot mustard or sweet and sour sauce. Makes 8 to 10 egg rolls.

Shrimp and Black Bean Chili

As delicious as it is colorful, this Texas chili features our favorite seafood and a medley of vegetables in a savory and spicy broth.

1 pound small to medium shrimp, about 31/35 count
1 medium chopped onion
1 tablespoon canola oil
1 can (16 ounces) black beans, drained and rinsed
1 can (1 pound 12 ounces) whole tomatoes, cut up, with juice

1 cup fish stock or chicken broth
1 green bell pepper, cut in 1" pieces
1 yellow bell pepper, cut in 1" pieces
1/3 cup prepared picante sauce
1 teaspoon cumin
1/2 teaspoon basil

In a large Dutch oven or stew pot, saute onion in oil until tender. Add remaining ingredients except shrimp and cook over medium heat for 10 minutes. Add shrimp and simmer for 5 minutes. Serve with grated cheese and hot Mexican cornbread. Makes 4 to 6 servings.

Shrimp and Black Bean Chili, page 48

Sauteed Shrimp with Peppers and Cream

Originally from Ruggles Grill in Houston, this is our version of a spicy and quick saute of shrimp from Virginia Elverson's book, **Gulf Coast Cooking**.

18 large shrimp, at least 16/20s
2 tablespoons canola or olive oil
2 cloves minced garlic
2 tablespoons grated ginger root
1/4 cup dry white wine
1/4 cup heavy cream

4 tablespoons finely chopped jalapeño peppers
1/4 cup chopped fresh cilantro
Juice from 1 fresh lime
Dash of salt and white pepper

In a skillet, heat oil and saute garlic and ginger root. Add shrimp, and cook, stirring constantly for 1 minute or until shrimp begin to turn opaque. Whisk in wine and cook until most of wine evaporates. Add cream and cook on low heat until liquid is reduced. Add chopped jalapeños, cilantro, lime juice, salt and pepper. Makes 4 servings.

Pickled Shrimp

This is a must for buffets and special occasions. It's easy, delicious and even better on the second or third day. Double or triple the recipe.

2 pounds raw, peeled and deveined shrimp, 41-50 count or larger
2 medium white or purple onions, sliced into rings
1 cup vegetable oil

1 1/2 cups white vinegar
1/2 cup sugar
1 1/2 teaspoons salt
1 1/2 teaspoons celery seeds
4 tablespoons capers with juice

Place shrimp in boiling salted water, reduce heat and simmer for 3 to 5 minutes. Shrimp are done when they are pink and tender. Drain and rinse with cold water, then chill. Make alternate layers of shrimp and onion rings in a sealable container. Mix remaining ingredients and pour over shrimp and onions. Seal and place in refrigerator for 8 to 24 hours, shaking or inverting occasionally. Drain and serve. Makes 6 servings.

The iodine taste in shrimp is the result of wild shrimp (usually brown) feeding on dead plants and taking on a strong flavor of bromphenol, a natural byproduct of aquatic plants.

Shrimp Puppies, page 47

Texas Grilled Shrimp

Try an outdoor Texas barbecue with the biggest shrimp you can find and all the trimmings.

1 1/2 pounds under-10 count, Texas shrimp
1/4 cup olive oil
2 cloves minced garlic
Juice of 1 lemon

1 tablespoon cracked black pepper
2 tablespoons chopped fresh parsley
15 slices lean bacon

Mix oil, garlic, lemon juice, pepper and parsley together in flat pan. Marinate shrimp in oil mixture for 1 hour. Prepare grill. Cut excess fat off ends of bacon slices. Wrap a slice of bacon around each shrimp and fasten with a wooden pick. Grill shrimp on medium heat for 5 minutes, turning and basting once. Shrimp are done when opaque throughout. Do not over cook. Discard bacon and serve shrimp with slaw, red beans and cornbread. Makes 4 to 5 servings. (Pictured opposite page 56)

Shrimp Cantonese

An easy preparation method to star shrimp and crisp, colorful vegetables at your next meal.

2 pounds peeled and deveined Texas shrimp
2 tablespoons olive oil
2 cups each diagonally sliced celery and carrots
2 cups sliced onion
1/4 cup finely chopped red bell pepper

8 ounces fresh spinach leaves
2 cups fresh bean sprouts
1 1/4 cups chicken broth
1/4 cup soy sauce
1/4 teaspoon pepper
3 tablespoons cornstarch
3 cups cooked hot rice

Saute shrimp in oil for one minute or until they begin to turn pink. Add celery, carrots, onion, bell pepper and cook over medium heat, stirring constantly, for 2 minutes. Add spinach and bean sprouts. Cook for one minute. In a separate container, blend broth, soy sauce, pepper and cornstarch. Stir gently into mixture and heat thoroughly until broth thickens. Serve over hot rice. Makes 6 servings.

Sweet and Sour Shrimp

The delicate flavor of Gulf shrimp is teamed with a tangy sauce, then served on hot rice.

1 pound peeled and deveined Texas shrimp
1 1/2 cups apple juice
1/2 cup vinegar
1/4 cup sugar
1/4 cup ketchup
2 tablespoons melted margarine
1 tablespoon soy sauce
1/4 teaspoon salt

1/2 cup diagonally sliced carrots
1/2 cup cubed green pepper
1/4 cup sliced green onions and tops
2 tablespoons cornstarch
1/4 cup apple juice
1/2 cup toasted, slivered almonds
Hot cooked rice

In a skillet or wok, combine apple juice, vinegar, sugar, ketchup, margarine, soy sauce and salt. Bring to a boil and add shrimp, carrots, peppers and onions. Cover and simmer for 15 minutes. In a small container, dissolve cornstarch in apple juice. Add gradually to hot mixture and cook until thickened stirring constantly. Add almonds to rice and serve shrimp sauce over rice. Makes 6 servings.

Texas Shrimp Boil

A pile of you-peel-'em Texas shrimp — now that's good eating!

2 pounds Texas shrimp tails (at least 26-30 count)
1 1/2 ounces prepared shrimp boil
1 small sliced onion

1 sliced lemon
1 clove sliced garlic
2 tablespoons salt
Rockport Red Sauce

Place 1 1/2 quarts water in large boiler pot. Add remaining ingredients except shrimp. Cover and bring to a boil. Add shrimp and return to a boil. Reduce heat and simmer for 3 minutes, until shrimp are tender. Drain. Serve with Rockport Red Sauce. Makes 2 to 3 servings. To make **ROCKPORT RED SAUCE** combine 1 cup chili sauce or ketchup, 3 tablespoons lemon juice, 1 tablespoon horseradish, 3 drops liquid hot pepper sauce, 1/2 teaspoon celery salt, 1/8 teaspoon salt. Chill well. Makes approximately 1 cup sauce.

For a change of pace, serve boiled shrimp and grilled or broiled scallops with several fresh salsas instead of seafood sauce.

Shrimp Victoria

Versatile Texas shrimp becomes gourmet fare in minutes when cooked in mushrooms, butter, sour cream and seasonings.

1 pound peeled and deveined Texas shrimp, about 26-30 count
1/2 cup finely chopped onion
1/4 cup margarine or butter
1 can (6 ounces) sliced mushrooms or 1 cup sliced fresh mushrooms

1 tablespoon flour
1/4 teaspoon salt
Dash cayenne pepper
1 cup sour cream or plain yogurt
1 1/2 cups hot cooked rice

Saute shrimp and onion in margarine for 5 minutes or until shrimp are tender. Add mushrooms and cook for 2 to 3 minutes more. Sprinkle in flour, salt and pepper. Stir in sour cream and cook gently for 10 minutes, being careful to keep heat low. Serve over rice. Makes 4 to 6 servings.

Shrimp Sauce and Spaghetti Squash

A low fat winner featuring delicious Texas shrimp and a squash accompaniment.

1 1/2 pounds raw, peeled and deveined Texas shrimp, 31-35 count or smaller
1 medium spaghetti squash, 3 to 3 1/2 pounds
1 tablespoon olive oil
1 cup minced onions
2 cloves minced garlic (optional)

1 teaspoon freshly ground black pepper
1/2 cup dry white wine
1/2 teaspoon hot red pepper flakes
1/3 cup chopped fresh parsley
1 tablespoon fresh lemon juice
1 tablespoon margarine

Cut squash in half lengthwise and discard seeds. Bake both halves, cut side down, for 35 to 40 minutes at 350 degrees. Or, place whole squash in a steamer and steam for 15 minutes. Squash should be tender when pressed or pierced with a fork. Set aside. In a skillet, add olive oil and shrimp and saute for 1 minute. Add onions and garlic and cook until they are soft, about 1 minute more. Add remaining ingredients except margarine and simmer for 2 minutes. Remove from heat. With a fork, "comb" out the yellow flesh of the squash, working from the cut edges toward the center to produce long spaghetti-like strands. Reheat squash in saucepan, stirring in margarine if desired. At the same time, reheat shrimp sauce, but do not boil. To serve, spoon sauce over spaghetti squash. Makes 4 servings.

Shrimp Gumbo, page 58

Shrimp Ratatouille

This classic French vegetable stew is enhanced and made hearty with tender delectable Texas shrimp. It is low in calories but very filling.

1 pound raw, peeled and deveined
  Texas shrimp, 31-35 count
1/4 cup olive oil
1 cup thinly sliced zucchini
1 small eggplant, peeled or unpeeled
  and cut into 1-inch pieces
1/2 cup thinly sliced onion
1 medium green pepper, cut into 1-
  inch pieces

1 cup sliced fresh mushrooms
1 can (1 pound) tomato wedges
1 1/2 teaspoons garlic salt
1 teaspoon crushed basil
1 tablespoon chopped fresh parsley
1/4 teaspoon pepper

Cut shrimp in half lengthwise. In large skillet, saute zucchini, eggplant, onion, green pepper and mushrooms in oil for 5 minutes or until tender-crisp. Add shrimp, stirring frequently for about 2 minutes. Add tomatoes, garlic salt, basil, parsley and pepper. Cover and simmer about 5 minutes or until shrimp are tender. Serve with rice or noodles. Makes 6 servings.

Shrimp Potato Boats

A special treat for baked potato lovers. You will love the taste of Texas Shrimp combined with other potato favorites.

1 pound peeled and cooked Texas
  shrimp, coarsely chopped
4 large baking potatoes
1/2 cup margarine
1/2 cup half-and-half cream
1/4 cup chopped green onions and
  tops

1 cup grated sharp cheese
1/2 teaspoon salt
Paprika
Fresh parsley

Scrub potatoes thoroughly. Bake at 425 degrees for 45 minutes or in the microwave oven according to your oven instructions. When cool to touch, cut potatoes in half lengthwise or remove just the top third. Scoop out pulp, leaving a firm shell about 1/4 inch thick. Combine potato pulp, margarine, half-and-half, onion, cheese and salt. Whip until smooth. Stir in shrimp. Stuff shells with shrimp mixture and sprinkle with paprika. Bake at 425 degrees for 10 minutes. Garnish with parsley. Makes 4 servings.

Shrimp Hurry Curry

A top-of-the-range main dish prepared in minutes with economical small shrimp, can soups, sour cream and curry.

1 1/2 pounds raw, peeled and deveined Texas shrimp, 31-35 count or smaller
2 tablespoons margarine
1 can (10 1/2 ounces) condensed cream of shrimp soup
1 can (10 1/2 ounces) condensed cream of mushroom soup

3/4 cup sour cream or plain yogurt
1 1/2 teaspoons curry powder
2 tablespoons chopped fresh parsley
Rice, toast points, or patty shells

In a skillet, saute shrimp in margarine for 3 to 5 minutes over low heat, stirring frequently. Add soups and stir until thoroughly blended. Stir in sour cream, curry powder and parsley. Continue stirring until mixture is hot, then serve immediately on hot rice, toast points or in patty shells. Makes 4 to 6 servings.

Curried Shrimp and Rice

With a taste of cuisine from India, shrimp with apple and raisins are combined and served over rice or in crepes. A chunky sweet version of the recipe above.

1 pound peeled and deveined shrimp, 31-35 count
2 tablespoons margarine
1/2 cup finely chopped celery
1/4 cup finely chopped onion
1 1/2 cups finely chopped, peeled raw apple

1/4 cup seedless raisins
1 can (10 3/4 ounces) condensed cream of shrimp soup
1/2 teaspoon curry powder
1 teaspoon lemon juice
Hot cooked rice

Cut shrimp in half, lengthwise and rinse. In a skillet, saute shrimp, celery and onion in margarine until nearly done, about 3 minutes. Stir in apple, raisins, undiluted soup, curry powder and lemon juice. Heat thoroughly, mixing well. Serve over hot, cooked rice. Makes 4 hearty servings.

Why are some shrimp sweeter than others? Shrimp grown at higher salinities have higher free amino acid levels in the muscle which may result in a sweeter taste.

Curry Baked Shrimp

Tender shrimp are dipped in egg, then rolled in bread crumbs and spiced with curry for an exotic taste. Leave out the curry for a plainer oven-fried shrimp.

2 pounds peeled and deveined
   shrimp, 21-25 count
1 beaten egg
1 cup toasted bread crumbs

2 teaspoons curry powder
1/2 teaspoon salt
1/8 teaspoon pepper
1/4 cup vegetable oil

In a flat dish, combine egg and 1 tablespoon water. In another dish, combine crumbs, curry powder, salt and pepper. Dip shrimp in egg, then roll in crumb mixture. Place on a well-greased baking sheet. Drizzle oil sparingly over shrimp. Bake at 350 degrees for 5 to 7 minutes or until shrimp is golden brown. Makes 6 servings. Good served with a **SWEET-SOY DIP**. To make dip, combine 1/3 cup orange marmalade, 1/4 cup lemon juice, 1/4 cup soy sauce, 1 clove minced garlic and a dash of ginger in a small saucepan. Bring to a boil. Dissolve 1 teaspoon cornstarch in 1 tablespoon water. Add to hot sauce and cook until slightly thickened, stirring constantly. Serve hot. Makes approximately 2/3 cup sauce.

Shrimp de Jonghe

This stretchable shrimp delight is tossed with lightly seasoned bread crumbs and baked conventionally or via microwaves.

1 pound peeled and deveined Texas
   shrimp, 31-35 count or smaller
1 cup toasted dry bread crumbs
1/4 cup chopped green onions and
   tops
1/4 cup chopped parsley
2 cloves chopped garlic

3/4 teaspoon crushed tarragon
1/4 teaspoon nutmeg
1/4 teaspoon salt
Dash pepper
1/2 cup melted margarine
1/4 cup sherry

In a large mixing bowl, combine crumbs, onions, parsley and remaining ingredients, except shrimp, in order listed. Mix thoroughly. Add shrimp to crumb mixture and toss lightly. Place in a well-greased casserole and cover with aluminum foil. Bake at 350 degrees for 25 minutes or until shrimp is done and crumbs are lightly browned. Remove foil during last 15 minutes of cooking. To cook in the microwave oven, bake for 10 minutes on HIGH turning dish once. Makes 6 servings.

Shrimp and Pasta Vinaigrette

A surprise taste sensation! Cooked skillet style, Texas shrimp and shell pasta are complemented by a pleasantly tart and aromatic vinaigrette.

1 1/2 pounds peeled and deveined shrimp
1 cup uncooked macaroni sea shells
3 tablespoons olive or canola oil
3/4 cup chopped onion
2 chopped garlic cloves
1/3 cup white vinegar
1/2 teaspoon sugar
1/2 teaspoon dry mustard
1/4 teaspoon dried oregano
1/4 teaspoon basil
1 1/4 cups sliced celery
1/2 cup sliced radishes
1 can (4 ounces) sliced black olives
8 ounces mozzarella cheese, cut into 1/2-inch cubes
Parmesan cheese

Cook macaroni according to package directions. Drain and set aside. In a deep skillet, heat oil. Add shrimp, onion and garlic and cook until shrimp begin to turn pink, about 3 minutes. In a small container, mix vinegar, sugar, mustard, oregano and basil and add to skillet. Add celery and cook on medium heat for 5 minutes. Reduce heat and stir in pasta, radishes, olives and cheese. Cover and heat just until cheese melts. Serve immediately. Sprinkle with Parmesan cheese. Serve with hot garlic-sesame bread. Pass additional Parmesan cheese. Makes 4 hearty servings.

Golden Fried Shrimp

Most shrimp lovers have a favorite fried shrimp recipe. If you don't, try this one.

1 1/2 pounds raw, shell-on shrimp, 26-30 count
2 beaten eggs
1 teaspoon salt
1/4 cup flour
1/2 cup crushed saltine crackers

Butterfly shrimp and wash under cold running water. Combine eggs and salt in a shallow bowl. Combine flour and cracker crumbs in flat pan. Dip each shrimp in egg mixture, then roll in cracker mixture. Repeat procedure. Fry at 365 degrees for 2 to 3 minutes or until golden brown. Drain on absorbent paper. Makes 4 to 6 servings.

Texas Grilled Shrimp, page 50

Farmer's Seafood Boil

A concoction of great Texas agricultural products. Double or triple for a large, hungry crowd.

2 pounds shell-on, headless
   shrimp, at least 26-30 count
2 packages (3 ounces each) crab
   and shrimp boil
2 tablespoons salt
12 whole new potatoes or 3 russet
   potatoes, unpared and quartered

4 onions, quartered
1 link pork or Italian sausage, cut
   into 1 1/2-inch pieces
3 ears corn, cut in thirds

In a large boiling pot, bring a gallon of water, crab and shrimp boil and salt to a boil. Add potatoes and boil for 10 minutes. Add onions and sausage and boil for 5 minutes. Add shrimp and corn. Boil for 5 minutes more. Drain and serve with crusty bread and a cold beverage. Makes 6 servings.

Creamy Shrimp Fettuccine

Tender shrimp added to a Bechamel sauce laced with wine and dill and served over green fettuccine. Put candles on your table for this one!

1 pound peeled and deveined
   shrimp, 26-30 count or smaller
5 tablespoons margarine
1 tablespoon chopped onion
3/4 cup white wine
1/2 teaspoon salt

3 tablespoons flour
1 1/2 cups milk
1 1/2 teaspoons chopped fresh dill
   or 3/4 teaspoon dried dill
2 teaspoons lemon juice
Green fettuccine

In a saucepan, heat 2 tablespoons margarine. Add onions, shrimp and wine and cook for 5 minutes. In a separate saucepan, melt the remaining margarine. Add the flour and stir until blended. Gradually add milk to the mixture, stirring vigorously until the sauce is thick and smooth. Add the sauce and dill to the shrimp mixture and simmer for 5 minutes. Serve over fettuccine. Makes 4 servings.

Chunky Shrimp Salad

As healthful as it is colorful, this high fiber shrimp and vegetable salad is balanced for nutrition, flavor and eye appeal.

1 pound cooked and peeled 26-30 count shrimp
4 ounces cubed part skim Mozzarella cheese
1 can (15 ounces) garbanzos (chick peas), drained and rinsed
1 can (4 ounces) whole, pitted black olives
2 cups fresh broccoli florets

1 cup sliced fresh mushrooms
1/2 cup each sliced carrots, celery, and onions
1 package (10 ounces) frozen green peas
3 tablespoons chopped fresh parsley
Vinaigrette or creamy dressing
Salad greens

In a large mixing bowl, combine all salad ingredients and mix thoroughly. Portion salad in individual bowls or in a large serving bowl. Garnish with greens. To keep calorie count low, toss with a vinaigrette. Or, choose your favorite creamy dressing if preferred. Makes 6 servings.

Shrimp Gumbo

A southern culinary masterpiece with charm and flavor as unique as New Orleans.

2 pounds raw, peeled shrimp
1 pound flaked crab meat
1/3 cup flour
1/3 cup canola oil
2 cups chopped onions
2 cups chopped celery
1 cup chopped bell pepper
1 package (10 ounces) frozen cut okra
1 can (8 ounces) tomato sauce
1/4 cup chopped fresh parsley

1 can (13 ounces) chicken broth or fresh fish stock
3 bay leaves
2 tablespoons Worcestershire sauce
1 tablespoon thyme
2 tablespoons Kitchen Bouquet
2 teaspoons each garlic salt and pepper
Liquid hot pepper sauce to taste
Hot cooked rice

To make roux, heat oil in large cast-iron kettle, if available. When very hot, but not smoking, add half the flour. Stir constantly with wire whisk. Add remaining flour. Stir rapidly with whisk until dark and smooth. Add vegetables and cook until tender. Add tomato sauce, 3 cups water or fish or shrimp stock and chicken broth. Simmer for 1 hour. Add shrimp and remaining ingredients except rice. Simmer for 15 minutes. Serve over hot rice. Makes 8 to 10 servings.

Chunky Shrimp Salad, page 58

Fiesta Shrimp Casserole

A Tex-Mex concoction yielding a rich and hearty meal. Serve with a picante sauce.

3 cups cooked and peeled 31-35 count shrimp
3 corn tortillas, cut into eighths
1 envelope (1 1/4 ounces) dry onion soup mix
1 can (10 ounces) enchilada sauce
1 can (10 3/4 ounces) cream of chicken soup
1 can (4 ounces) chopped green chilies
1/2 cup chopped onions
1 can (4 ounces) sliced ripe olives
1/2 cup sliced or whole pimiento-stuffed, green olives
1 cup shredded Cheddar cheese
1/2 cup chopped pecans
1/2 cup raisins

Line a 14x8x2 inch casserole dish with corn tortilla wedges. In a saucepan, combine soup mix, 1/2 cup water, enchilada sauce, cream of chicken soup and green chilies. Heat thoroughly. Pour half of the sauce over the tortilla pieces. Arrange half of the shrimp over the sauce. Sprinkle with onions. Pour remaining sauce over the onions. Mix together olives, cheese, pecans and raisins and sprinkle over casserole. Bake for 20 minutes at 350 degrees. Arrange remaining shrimp on top. Return to oven for 5 minutes. Remove and let sit for 5 minutes before serving. Serve with a light salad if desired. Makes 6 servings.

Shrimp Alamo

A tribute to the siege of the Alamo — Texans' favorite seafood with Mexican flavored rice.

1 1/2 pounds peeled and cleaned shrimp, 26-30 count
1 cup raw, long-grained rice
3 tablespoons canola oil
1 medium chopped tomato
1/2 cup chopped onion
1 can (10 ounces) tomatoes and chilies
1/4 cup chopped fresh parsley
1/4 teaspoon each salt and pepper
1/4 teaspoon cumin

In a large skillet cook rice in oil until rice is golden brown, about 5 minutes. Add two cups water and remaining ingredients except shrimp. Cover and cook for 8 minutes. Add shrimp and cook for 5 minutes. Serve with guacamole, refried beans and warm tortillas for a hearty Mexican meal. Makes 6 servings.

Shrimp and Noodle Casserole

A little shrimp goes a long way when extended with noodles in a creamy blend of mushrooms, onions and cheese.

1 pound cooked, peeled and
   deveined Texas shrimp, any size
1 package (8 ounces) medium
   noodles
2 cans (10 3/4 ounces each) condensed cream of mushroom soup
1 cup sour cream
1/2 cup sliced green onions and
   tops

1/4 cup chopped green pepper
1/2 teaspoon dried dill weed
1/2 teaspoon pepper
1/4 teaspoon salt
1/2 cup shredded Cheddar cheese
1 medium size tomato, sliced
Dill weed or parsley sprigs for
   garnish

Cut large shrimp in half. Cook noodles as directed on package and drain well. In a large mixing bowl, combine noodles with soup, sour cream, onions, green pepper, dried dill weed, pepper and salt. Cut half of the shrimp into thirds and fold shrimp and cheese into noodle mixture. Spoon into a shallow baking dish. Cover tightly with aluminum foil and bake at 350 degrees for 20 minutes. Remove foil and arrange remaining shrimp in rows on top of casserole. Cover and return to oven for 5 minutes or until hot and bubbly. Garnish with tomato slices and fresh dill weed or parsley sprigs. Makes 6 servings.

Shrimp and Pea Salad

So simple and satisfying and a feast for the eyes, too. My choice for a quick lunch.

2 pounds peeled and deveined
   Texas shrimp, 31-35 count
1 package (10 ounces) frozen green
   peas

1 purple onion, sliced
3/4 cup prepared herb, vinegar and
   oil or Italian dressing
1/2 teaspoon celery seeds

Add shrimp to boiling water. Return to a boil, reduce heat and simmer for 3 to 4 minutes. Shrimp should be opaque throughout. Drain and cool immediately. In a large bowl combine shrimp, frozen peas and onion. In a small container mix dressing with celery seeds. Stir into shrimp mixture. Serve on lettuce as an appetizer or as a main dish. Peas will be sufficiently thawed by serving time. Serve with crackers or bread sticks. Makes 6 servings.

Shrimp Butter, page 26

Broiled Rock Shrimp Tails

The luxury of lobster for the price of shrimp. Try this when you can find rock shrimp.

1 1/2 pounds rock shrimp tails, split
   and cleaned
2/3 cup melted margarine or butter

Juice of 1 lemon
1 1/2 teaspoons garlic salt
Paprika

To split and clean rock shrimp, hold tail in hand with belly-side up and the tail-end pointed away from you. Insert lower blade of scissors or kitchen shears into the exposed vein for the full length of the tail and snip meat in half. Spread severed tail open to fully expose the sand vein, then rinse thoroughly under cold running water to remove vein. Place cleaned tails on a broiler pan, shell-side down. Combine butter, lemon and garlic salt and drizzle over shrimp. Sprinkle with paprika and broil about 4 inches from source of heat for 2 to 3 minutes. Makes 4 to 6 servings.

Shrimp and Wild Rice Stuffing

Try this for a side dish or stuffing for a trophy fish or bird for a special holiday. Works great in an electric skillet or on stove top.

1 pound peeled and deveined
   shrimp, 21-25 count
1/4 cup margarine
1/4 cup chopped celery
1/4 cup chopped onion
4 cups prepared wild rice
1 beaten egg

2 tablespoons milk
1 jar (2 ounces) pimiento
1/2 teaspoon thyme
1/4 teaspoon salt
2 tablespoons chopped, fresh
   parsley
Dash pepper

Cut shrimp in half if 26-30's or larger. Over moderate heat, melt margarine in a large skillet or stew pot, and cook celery, onions and shrimp for 2 minutes. Add cooked rice. Beat egg with milk and stir into mixture. Fold in remaining ingredients, and cook until shrimp is tender and white throughout, about 5 minutes. Makes 6 servings.

 The black (intestinal) vein in shrimp is safe to eat, but removing it improves the appearance.

Shrimp Confetti

A quick, on-the-run idea that is as colorful as it is good. You'll need a skillet with a lid.

1 1/2 pounds Texas shrimp, 21-25 count or smaller
1 cup raw long grain rice (not instant)
1/2 cup sliced green onions and tops
1/4 cup cooking oil
1 can (13 ounces) chicken broth

1 1/2 teaspoons salt
1/4 teaspoon leaf thyme
Dash pepper
1 package (10 ounces) frozen peas, thawed
1/2 cup sliced pitted ripe olives
1 jar (2 ounces) pimiento

Peel and devein shrimp. In large skillet, heat rice and green onions in oil. Add chicken broth, 1/4 cup water, salt, thyme and pepper. Mix well. Bring to a boil. Cover and simmer for 15 minutes or until rice is nearly done. Add shrimp and remaining ingredients. Cover and cook over low heat for 5 minutes or until shrimp is done. Makes 6 servings.

Shrimp Tree St. Nick

Shrimp arranged on an endive covered cone makes a fun and edible center-piece.

3 pounds raw Texas shrimp, unpeeled, 26-30 count
2 quarts water
1/2 cup salt
4 large bunches curly endive

1 plastic foam cone, 2 1/2 feet high
1 plastic foam square, 12x12x1 inch
1 small box round toothpicks
Cocktail sauce

Place thawed shrimp in boiling salted water. Cover and simmer about 5 minutes or until shrimp are pink and tender. Peel shrimp, leaving the last section of shell on. Remove sand veins and wash. Chill. Separate and wash endive. Chill. Place cone on center of plastic foam square and draw a circle around the base. Cut out the circle and insert the cone. Cover base and cone with overlapping leaves of endive. Fasten endive to plastic cone with toothpick halves. Start at the outside edge of the base and work up. Cover fully with greens to resemble a Christmas tree. Attach shrimp to tree with toothpicks. Provide cocktail sauce for dipping shrimp.

 Head shrimp, but leave the shells on to offer extra insulation during freezing.

Teriyaki Shrimp

A fellow Girl Scout and seafood lover, Lynn Wilbur of Dallas, takes this recipe on camping trips with her troop. Lucky Scouts! Sure beats the same ole ground meat cowboy stews. This marinade is also a great light sauce to bake fish in.

2 pounds peeled and deveined
  shrimp
1/2 cup soy sauce
1/2 cup Japanese rice wine (Sake)

3 cloves finely chopped garlic
4 tablespoons sugar
1 teaspoon grated fresh ginger

Place all ingredients including shrimp in a zip-type bag. Place in the refrigerator for at least 2 hours or pack in a cooler with ice if you are going on a trip. Then remove shrimp and cook by grilling or stir frying with vegetables of your choice cut julienne. Makes 4 to 6 servings.

Pesto With Shrimp and Pasta

This recipe was given to me by a seafood lover I met while demonstrating seafood preparation in a Dallas supermarket. It is a traditional sauce for pasta—this one with shrimp!

1 pound peeled and deveined shrimp
2 cups fresh basil leaves, lightly
  packed
1/2 cup Parmesan cheese

1/4 cup olive oil
3 cloves minced garlic
2 tablespoons pine nuts or walnuts
Hot cooked pasta

Wash and pat dry basil leaves. Place in a food processor or blender along with the cheese, oil and garlic. Process until the leaves are finely chopped. Add nuts and process briefly until nuts are ground, but not paste-like. Cook shrimp for 5 minutes in simmering water. Cut into bite-size pieces. In a large serving bowl, combine pesto, shrimp and hot pasta. Add a little olive oil if too dry. Makes 6 servings.

 Top your favorite pizza with a pound of cooked and chopped shrimp.

Grilled Shrimp With Avocado and Chili Pepper Sauce

The current president of International Association of Culinary Professionals, shared this recipe with us through her writings. Leslie Beal Bloom developed this sauce with grilled shrimp in mind, but it is also delicious on grilled fish.

2 pounds headed Texas shrimp, about 21-25 count
1 cup mashed avocado
1 whole chili pepper, softened in water
1 tablespoon plus 2 teaspoons fresh lime juice

2 teaspoons white-wine vinegar
1/2 cup plain nonfat yogurt
1 1/2 teaspoons cumin
1 teaspoon salt
1/4 cup plus 2 tablespoons olive oil
1/2 cup firmly packed fresh coriander

While shrimp is grilling, prepare the sauce. In a blender, puree the avocado, chili, lime juice, vinegar, yogurt, cumin, salt, oil, and coriander. Pulse the motor until the coriander is chopped. Serve the sauce at room temperature with grilled shrimp. Makes 2 cups sauce.

Shrimp and Cheese Grits

My version of a unique shrimp dish offered by Bon Appetit from Crook's Corner in Chapel Hill, North Carolina.

1 1/2 pounds peeled and deveined, 31-35 count shrimp
1/2 teaspoon salt
2 cups quick-cooking grits
1 cup grated sharp Cheddar cheese
1/4 teaspoon liquid hot pepper sauce

Pinch nutmeg
8 slices chopped bacon
1/2 pound sliced fresh mushrooms
1 cup sliced green onions
3 cloves minced garlic
2 tablespoons fresh lemon juice
1/4 cup chopped fresh parsley

In large saucepan, bring 6 cups water and salt to a boil. Whisk in grits and reduce heat. Cover and simmer until mixture is thick and grits are tender, about 10 minutes. Fold in cheese, hot sauce and nutmeg. Cover and set aside. In a large skillet, cook bacon until crisp. Remove bacon and pour off all but 1 tablespoon of bacon grease. Add shrimp, mushrooms, onion and garlic to same skillet and cook for 4 minutes on medium heat. Add cooked bacon, lemon juice, parsley and season to taste with salt and pepper. Reheat grits, adding a little water if too thick. Portion grits onto plates and spoon shrimp mixture over. Makes four to six servings.

Calamari Rings (Squid)

With a dry coating and a short cooking time, fresh squid makes a juicy and crisp hors d'oeuvre.

3 pounds squid, cleaned and cut
   into rings
2 cups flour

1/4 teaspoon each salt and pepper
Oil for frying

Dry the squid with absorbent towels. Combine flour, salt and pepper. Coat squid with flour mixture. Heat peanut or canola oil to 365 degrees. Deep fry a few rings at a time until golden brown, about 2 minutes. Do not overcook. Drain on absorbent towels. Serve hot with horseradish, sweet and sour sauce or a teriyaki sauce. Makes 4 servings. (Pictured opposite page 66)

Stir Fried Calamari

This favorite of my family was inspired by Janis Harsila and Evie Hansen in **Seafood: A Collection of Heart Healthy Recipes**. Look for their book series. Every recipe is a winner.

1 pound cleaned squid
2 tablespoons light soy sauce
1/8 teaspoon pepper
2 tablespoons white wine
2 teaspoons cornstarch
1 tablespoon sesame oil
1 tablespoon canola oil

1 teaspoon grated fresh ginger
2 cloves minced garlic
1 cup sliced mushrooms
1 medium red or green pepper, cut
   julienne
1/4 cup sliced green onions and tops
1/2 cup frozen peas

Clean squid. Cut mantles (bodies) crosswise into 1/4 inch strips and chop tentacles. To make marinade combine soy sauce, pepper, wine, cornstarch and sesame oil. Mix well. Add squid and marinate at room temperature while preparing remaining ingredients. In large skillet or wok, heat oil. Add ginger and garlic. Stir fry for 30 seconds. Add squid and vegetables with marinade. Stir-fry briefly until squid is just cooked through, approximately 45 seconds. Serve immediately over hot rice. Makes 4 servings.

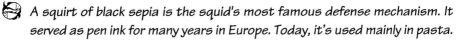 A squirt of black sepia is the squid's most famous defense mechanism. It served as pen ink for many years in Europe. Today, it's used mainly in pasta.

Mediterranean Calamari Salad

Vienna-born Perla Meyers, cooking teaching and author, endorses the use of fresh, high-quality foods and simple preparations. She brings the natural approach to the kitchen and to us through **Simply Seafood** magazine. Look for it in grocery stores and news stands!

1 1/2 pounds cleaned squid, including tentacles
5 tablespoons fresh lime juice
3 tablespoons red wine vinegar
1/4 cup olive oil
3 large cloves crushed and peeled garlic
1 teaspoon dried oregano or 1 tablespoon minced fresh

1/8 teaspoon cayenne pepper
1 red bell pepper, cut julienne
1 thinly sliced jalapeño pepper
3/4 cup fresh cilantro leaves
1/2 cup minced green onions and tops
Lettuce leaves

Cut squid into 1/2 inch rings. Steam or simmer for 30 seconds to 1 minute, no longer. Set aside. In a large mixing bowl, combine lime juice and vinegar. Slowly whisk in oil until well blended. Add garlic, oregano and cayenne. Season with salt and pepper. Add squid, red pepper, jalapeño, cilantro and onions. Toss, cover and chill for at least 4 hours. Portion on lettuce leaves for serving. Garnish with lemon slices and cilantro if desired.

Squid Facts

- The color of fresh squid should be mottled white or ivory and the odor mildly sweet, not "fishy".

- The fresher the squid, the more easily the pen or "backbone" detaches from the body.

- Frozen squid is very acceptable. Don't hesitate to buy it.

- Fresh or thawed squid should be placed in a plastic bag on ice in the refrigerator. Eat within two days.

- The tentacles are edible, too. Just chop them up and use with the main body part.

Boiled Crawfish

The taste of pond-raised crawfish is hard to beat when boiled in hot, spicy water.

12 to 15 pounds live crawfish
1 package (3 ounce) crab and
   shrimp boil mix

1 cup salt
2 tablespoons cayenne pepper

In a 10 gallon stew pot, bring water, crab boil, salt and pepper to a boil. Add crawfish and boil for 10 minutes. Remove from heat and let crawfish soak for 10 minutes. This allows meat to absorb flavors, so do not shorten soaking time. Drain and serve immediately. Makes 4 to 6 servings.

Crawfish Etouffee

Doyle and Ann Schaer are busy people who own and operate a successful crawfish farm in east Texas. This is their favorite quick etouffee recipe that tastes like it took all day to make.

2 pounds peeled, raw crawfish tails
1/3 cup vegetable oil
1/3 cup flour
3/4 cup chopped bell pepper
1 cup chopped green onions and
   tops
1 cup chopped celery

1/4 cup chopped fresh parsley
1 can (10 1/2 ounces) cream of
   celery soup
1/2 teaspoon Tony Chachere's
   Seasoning
1 teaspoon salt
Cayenne pepper to taste

In a heavy skillet, preferably cast iron, prepare a roux by combining oil and flour over low heat. Stir constantly until the roux is deep brown in color. This takes several minutes. Add vegetables and crawfish tails and combine thoroughly. Blend in 3 cups water and soup. Add seasonings and simmer for 30 minutes. Taste and adjust seasonings. Serve over hot rice. Makes 4 to 6 servings.

Crawfish Jambalaya

Based on the elements of French and Spanish cooking, this cousin of paella is great featuring crawfish.

2 pounds cooked and peeled
  crawfish
2 tablespoons margarine
3/4 cup chopped onion
1/2 cup chopped celery
1/4 cup chopped green pepper
1 tablespoon chopped fresh parsley
2 cloves minced garlic
1 cup cubed, fully cooked ham
  (optional)

1 can (28 ounces) tomatoes,
  undrained, cut up
1 can (10 1/2 ounces) chicken broth
1 1/4 cups water
1 cup uncooked long grain rice
1 teaspoon sugar
1/2 teaspoon crushed dried thyme
  leaves
1/2 teaspoon chili powder
1/4 teaspoon pepper

In electric skillet or Dutch oven, melt margarine. Add onion, celery, green pepper, parsley and garlic. Cover and cook until tender. Add remaining ingredients except crawfish. Cover, leaving lid vents open, and simmer for 20 minutes or until rice is tender. Add crawfish and heat throughout. Makes 6 servings.

Texas Oyster Nachos

If you like nachos, you'll be hooked on this Brazoria county original.

1 pint shucked oysters and shells
  or shell stock oysters
Broken, salted tortilla chips
1/2 cup spicy red sauce

1/2 cup grated cheese
Sliced jalapeño peppers
Rock salt
Oyster Shells

Drain oysters or shuck fresh ones. Pour rock salt in an ovenproof pan. Position clean shells in rock salt to steady them and to insulate the nachos. Place a few chip pieces in each shell, then an oyster on top. Add a dollop of red sauce and some grated cheese. Broil until the cheese melts and the edges of oysters curl. Top each nacho with a jalapeño slice. Serve hot, then make another batch. Makes 4 generous servings.

Oysters in Pecan and Bran Crust, page 69

Angels on Horseback

Savory hot hors d'oeuvres of bacon-wrapped oysters, lightly seasoned and broiled to perfection. For variety, try this with shrimp.

1 pint fresh oysters
Bacon slices, cut in thirds
1/4 cup chopped fresh parsley

1/2 teaspoon garlic salt
Wooden picks

Drain oysters. Place an oyster on each piece of bacon. Sprinkle with parsley and garlic salt. Wrap bacon around oyster and secure with a wooden pick. Place "angels" on broiler rack, about 4 inches from heat source, and broil 3 to 4 minutes. Turn carefully and broil on other side if desired. Cook only until bacon is done, being careful not to overcook oysters. Makes about 25 hors d'oeuvres. (*Pictured opposite page 68*)

Oysters In Pecan and Bran Crust

This adaptation is from my friend, Master Chef Victor Gielisse of Actuelle in Dallas, where seafood is a specialty.

1 pint fresh shucked oysters
1 1/2 cups flour
1/2 teaspoon salt
1/4 teaspoon pepper

2 lightly beaten eggs
2 cups finely chopped pecans
2 cups bran flakes
Canola oil for pan frying

Combine flour, salt and pepper. In a three-step process, coat each oyster in flour, beaten eggs and nut-bran mixture. Fry in hot oil about a minute on each side, or until oysters are a rich brown color. Drain and serve immediately. Makes 6 servings.

Seafood Stuffed Mushrooms

A delicious blend of fresh mushrooms and a savory seafood stuffing to enhance a party or special dinner.

1 cup cooked, flaked fish, crab meat or chopped shrimp
24 large mushrooms
2 tablespoons margarine
2 tablespoons each finely chopped onion and celery

1 cup fresh whole wheat bread crumbs
1 tablespoon chopped pimiento
1 tablespoon mayonnaise
1 tablespoon fresh lemon juice
1/8 teaspoon each cayenne and salt

Remove stems from clean mushrooms. Brush mushroom caps with oil and place on a baking sheet. Finely chop half the stems and saute in margarine with onion and celery. In a small mixing bowl, combine sauteed vegetables with remaining ingredients. Stuff each mushroom cap. Sprinkle with paprika and bake at 350 degrees for 5 minutes.

Seafood Chalupas

A tasty way to use a bit of leftover seafood—combined with a myriad of ingredients to create a quick Mexican treat.

1 cup leftover or fresh cooked fish, crab meat or shrimp
4 crisp, flat tortillas
1 can (8 ounces) refried beans

2 cups shredded lettuce
1 chopped tomato
1/2 cup grated Cheddar cheese
Salsa, avocado slices

To crispen tortillas, bake at 350 degrees for 3 minutes. Spread beans on each tortilla. Then layer with seafood, lettuce, tomato and cheese. Pass the salsa and sliced avocados. Makes 2 servings of 2 chalupas each.

Make a crab meat substitute by poaching a coarse textured fish like king mackerel in crab boil.

Seafood Chalupas, page 70

Golden Fried Oysters, page
71

Oysters Rockefeller

A classic named after John D. Rockefeller, this 1899 New Orleans recipe features oysters in a flavorful way.

1 pint large fresh oysters (approximately 18)
1/4 cup margarine or butter
1/4 cup chopped celery
1/4 cup chopped green onions including tops
2 tablespoons chopped parsley
1 package (10 ounces) frozen, chopped spinach, defrosted

1 peeled garlic clove
1 tablespoon fresh lemon juice
1/4 teaspoon anisette (optional)
1/4 teaspoon salt
Rock salt
18 oyster shells or ramekins
1/4 cup dry bread crumbs
1 tablespoon melted margarine or butter

In small saucepan, saute celery, onions and parsley in margarine until tender. In blender, combine sauteed vegetables, spinach, garlic, lemon juice, anisette and salt. Blend until almost pureed. When necessary, stop blender and push vegetables into blades. Fill a shallow, oven-proof serving dish with rock salt. Nest oyster shells into salt bed which holds shells in place and keeps oysters hot. Place the oysters in the shells. Top each oyster with spinach mixture. Combine bread crumbs and melted margarine, and sprinkle crumb mixture over oysters. Bake at 450 degrees for 10 minutes. Serve immediately. Makes 6 appetizer servings of 3 oysters each.

Golden Fried Oysters

A popular way to enjoy one of the bay's most treasured flavors.

24 fresh shucked oysters
2 egg whites, 1 egg yolk
2 tablespoons milk
1 teaspoon seasoned salt

1/4 teaspoon black pepper
1 cup yellow cornmeal
1/2 cup flour
Canola oil for frying

Drain oysters. Combine eggs, milk and seasonings. Dip oysters in egg mixture and roll in dry mixture. Repeat process to form double breading. Heat oil to 365 degrees. Fry oysters 2 to 3 minutes until golden brown. Makes 4 servings of 6 oysters each.

Nutty Oyster Balls

This unique item offers good flavor and interesting texture. Your friends will want the recipe.

1 pint fresh oysters
1/4 cup blanched, toasted slivered
   almonds
1 beaten egg
1 tablespoon chopped onion
1 tablespoon chopped fresh parsley

1/4 teaspoon salt
Dash nutmeg
Dash pepper
1/2 cup fine bread crumbs
Oil for frying
Wallace sauce

Drain oysters thoroughly. Chop oysters and almonds. Combine them with bread crumbs, egg, onion, parsley and seasonings. Mix thoroughly. Drop by tablespoonfuls into crumbs. Roll to form balls. Place in a single layer in a fry basket. Fry in hot oil, 365 degrees, for 2 to 3 minutes or until golden brown. Drain on absorbent paper. Makes approximately 30 hors d'oeuvres. To make **WALLACE SAUCE**: combine 1 cup light mayonnaise, 1 tablespoon prepared mustard and 2 teaspoons minced onion.

    Note: Oyster balls may be made ahead for later use. Fry as indicated, cool and store in vapor-proof bag or container and freeze. To heat, place frozen balls on baking sheet and bake at 400 degrees for 10 minutes or until heated throughout.

Anne's Golden Oyster Stew

A creamy and hearty revision of the basic stew. This one is full of surprises!

1 quart fresh oysters, undrained
1/2 cup chopped onion
1/2 cup sliced celery
2 tablespoons margarine
2 cups sliced fresh mushrooms
2 tablespoons flour
1/4 teaspoon salt
1/4 teaspoon pepper

2 cups milk
1 1/2 cups grated sharp Cheddar
   cheese
1 can (10 1/2 ounces) cream of
   potato soup
1 jar (2 ounces) diced pimiento
1/4 teaspoon liquid hot pepper
   sauce

Remove any remaining shell particles from oysters. In large sauce pan, cook onion and celery in margarine until tender. Add mushrooms and cook for 1 minute. Over low heat, whisk flour, salt and pepper into vegetable mixture. Add milk gradually until thickened, being careful not to boil. Add cheese and stir until melted. Add oysters, soup, pimiento and liquid hot pepper sauce. Over low heat, cook for 5 to 10 minutes or until oysters begin to curl. Makes 6 to 8 servings.

Oyster Artichoke Soup

This light broth creates a nutritious soup of oysters, artichokes and corn. Great year 'round.

1 pint oysters with liquid
2 tablespoons margarine
1/4 cup chopped green onions
2 cloves minced garlic
1/2 pound sliced fresh mushrooms
1/2 box (10-ounce box) frozen corn kernels
2 cups milk

1 can (8 1/2 ounces) drained and chopped artichoke hearts
2 tablespoons fresh lemon juice
2 dashes liquid hot pepper sauce
Salt and pepper to taste
1 beaten egg yolk, optional
Pinch of grated nutmeg

Simmer oysters and liquid in a skillet for about 1 minute, until edges of oysters curl. Remove oysters and cut in half. Add margarine to oyster liquid and heat. Add onions, garlic and mushrooms and saute for 5 minutes. Add corn and milk, stirring constantly. When milk begins to simmer, add chopped oysters, chopped artichokes, lemon juice, hot pepper sauce, salt and pepper and yolk, if desired. Be careful not to boil. Sprinkle with nutmeg. Makes 6 servings. (Pictured opposite page 74)

Oyster-Mushroom Stuffing

Lavish your imagination on a luscious creation of succulent oysters and a myriad of other ingredients—not for holidays only!

1 pint oysters
1 pound coarsely chopped mushrooms
1 1/2 cups chopped celery with leaves
1 cup chopped onion
1/2 cup margarine or butter
2 cups toasted whole wheat bread cubes

1/4 cup chopped fresh parsley
2 tablespoons diced pimiento
2 teaspoons salt
1 1/2 teaspoons poultry seasoning
1/4 teaspoon black pepper
2 beaten eggs

Remove any remaining shell particles from oysters. Drain oysters. In a skillet, saute mushrooms, celery and onion in margarine until tender but not brown. Place in a large mixing bowl and stir in bread cubes, parsley, pimiento and seasonings. Add oysters and eggs to mixture. Mix thoroughly. Makes approximately 6 cups stuffing. To serve as a side dish, place stuffing in a well-greased baking dish. Bake at 350 degrees for 20 minutes. Makes 6 to 8 servings.

Oysters Casino

This unique oyster recipe is destined to become one of your most popular hors d'oeuvres.

1 pint fresh oysters
1 cup frozen chopped spinach, thawed
1/2 cup grated Romano cheese

1/3 cup seasoned, toasted bread crumbs
18 1-inch squares of uncooked bacon
18 oyster shells

Arrange oyster shells in shallow, oven-proof serving dish. Squeeze excess liquid from spinach. Place one tablespoon of spinach inside each oyster shell. Top each bed of spinach with one large or two small oysters. Portion cheese evenly over oysters. Sprinkle with bread crumbs. Top each with a square of bacon. Broil for 3 to 4 minutes or until bacon is done. Serve hot. Makes 18 hors d'oeuvres. This recipe can also be preapred without the oyster shells.

Oysters Opulent

Feature the abundance of oysters in a bubbly hot casserole. The artichokes make it a treat, but you can use sliced zucchini for economy.

1 pint fresh oysters
1/4 cup margarine
1 cup chopped celery
2/3 cup chopped onion
2 sliced, hard-cooked eggs
1 can (7 1/2 ounces) artichoke hearts, cut in half

1 can (10 1/2 ounces) cream of mushroom soup
1/2 teaspoon salt
5 drops liquid hot pepper sauce
1 bay leaf
1/2 cup bread crumbs

Drain oysters. In saucepan, melt margarine and saute celery and onion until almost done. Add oysters and cook 2 to 3 minutes until edges curl. Stir in remaining ingredients except crumbs. Pour into casserole and top with bread crumbs. Bake uncovered at 350 degrees until mixture is bubbly and crumbs brown, about 15 minutes. Makes 6 servings. Sauce will be thin, so hot cooked rice or toast points are good accompaniments.

 Place an oyster or two in each compartment of an ice tray and fill with water. Freeze, pop out and store the oysters in a freezer bag for use a few at a time.

Oyster Artichoke Soup, page 73

Crab in Tomato Sauce with Pasta, page 75

Stuffed Soft-Shell Crab

A delicious preparation for the coveted soft shell crab.

8 cleaned soft-shell crabs
1/4 cup chopped onions
1/4 chopped celery
2 tablespoons chopped green
   peppers
1 clove minced garlic
1/4 cup melted margarine
1 cup rich cracker crumbs

2 tablespoons milk
1 beaten egg
1 tablespoon chopped fresh parsley
1/2 teaspoon dry mustard
1/2 teaspoon Worcestershire sauce
1/4 teaspoon salt
1/8 teaspoon cayenne pepper

Thaw crabs if frozen. Wash crabs thoroughly and drain. Cook onions, celery, green peppers and garlic in margarine until tender. In a medium bowl, combine mixture with next 8 ingredients. Place soft crabs in well-greased baking pan. Remove top shell from crabs and fill each cavity with 1 tablespoon stuffing. Replace top shell. Brush crabs with melted margarine. Bake at 400 degrees for 15 minutes. Makes 4 servings. To fry crabs, wash and dredge in seasoned flour and cornmeal. Deep fry at 365 degrees for 5 to 7 minutes.

Crab in Tomato Sauce With Pasta

Satisfying and good for you, fresh crab meat and spinach team up in a tomato sauce for a hearty topping on the pasta of your choice.

1 pound flaked blue crab meat
2 tablespoons margarine
1 tablespoon olive oil
1 medium coarsely chopped onion
3 cloves minced garlic
2 tablespoons flour
1 can (16 ounces) whole tomatoes,
   quartered and undrained

1 cup chicken broth
1/2 teaspoon salt
1/4 teaspoon pepper
4 cups fresh spinach leaves or 1
   package (10 ounces) frozen
   spinach, thawed
2/3 cup Parmesan cheese
Hot cooked spaghetti or linguine

In a large skillet, combine margarine and olive oil and saute onion and garlic over medium heat for 2 to 3 minutes. Add the flour and cook and stir until flour is well blended. Stir in tomatoes, broth, salt and pepper. Bring to a boil, reduce heat, cover and simmer for 10 minutes. Add crab meat and cook for 5 minutes. Stir in spinach and cook just until fresh spinach wilts or the packaged spinach is hot. Toss hot pasta with 1/3 cup Parmesan cheese then top pasta with crab-tomato sauce. Pass remaining cheese. Makes 4 to 6 servings.

Moss' Crab Au Gratin

This is very rich, but got so many compliments from a group of fisheries specialists that we decided to include it. Charles Moss made it famous in Galveston, Texas.

2 pounds lump crab meat
1/4 cup butter or margarine
1/4 cup flour
1 1/2 cups half-and-half
1/2 teaspoon dry mustard

1 cup grated Parmesan cheese
1/4 teaspoon each salt and pepper
2 beaten eggs
1 cup sliced, sauteed mushrooms
1/4 cup dry sherry

Place crab meat in a large mixing bowl and pick through to remove any remaining shell or cartilage. In small saucepan, combine butter, flour, cream, mustard and half of the Parmesan cheese. Heat and stir over moderate heat. Add salt and pepper. Mix some of the hot cream sauce into the eggs and add egg mixture back to remaining sauce. Gently fold sauce into the crab meat. Add mushrooms and sherry. Place in large casserole dish and sprinkle with remaining cheese. Bake at 400 degrees for approximately 20 minutes until casserole is bubbling hot. Makes 6 servings.

Sweet Potato Crab Cakes

We include this in our Thanksgiving buffet, but you can enjoy it anytime you have fresh crab meat.

1 pound flaked crab meat
3/4 cup cooked, whipped sweet
  potatoes
1 egg white
2 tablespoons mayonnaise
2 teaspoons lemon juice

1 tablespoon finely chopped onion
3 tablespoons finely chopped celery
1 clove finely minced garlic
1 cup dry, seasoned bread crumbs
2 tablespoons olive or canola oil

Place crab meat in large mixing bowl and pick through to remove any remaining shell or cartilage. Stir in potatoes, egg white, mayonnaise and lemon juice. In a small glass container, combine onion, celery, garlic and 1 tablespoon water. Microwave for 1 minute, then stir into potato mixture. Fold in crab meat. Shape crab mixture into 6 to 8 patties. Dredge each cake in bread crumbs. Heat oil and saute crab cakes until golden brown on each side. For a sweeter treat, sprinkle cakes with miniature marshmallows and bake in oven for 5 minutes just before serving. Makes 3 to 4 servings of two cakes each.

Crabmeat Stuffed Jalapeños

You will love these hot and savory peppers as an appetizer or as an accompaniment to a great meal.

1 pound flaked blue crab meat
1 can (1 pound 11 ounces) jalapeño
  peppers
2 tablespoons each, finely chopped
  green pepper, onions and dill
  pickle
1/4 cup cracker meal

1 beaten egg
1/4 teaspoon salt
1/4 teaspoon black pepper
1/8 teaspoon cayenne pepper
1 clove minced garlic
1/4 cup milk
Breading mixture

Cut peppers in half lengthwise. Discard pulp and seeds and rinse carefully. In a large mixing bowl, combine remaining ingredients except breading mixture. Stuff pepper halves with crab mixture and press stuffing around pepper. Set peppers aside. To prepare **Breading Mixture**, place 2 cups cracker meal in a flat pan. In a separate pan, mix 1 cup milk, 2 eggs and 1/4 teaspoon each salt and pepper. Dip peppers in egg mixture, then in cracker meal. Repeat procedure. Deep fry at 365 degrees until golden brown. Drain on absorbent paper. Makes 30 hors d'oeuvres. (Pictured opposite page 78)

Crab, Tomatillo and Corn Soup

A delicious and unusual soup made with delicate blue crab meat to create a comfort food for summer or winter.

8-10 ounces, flaked, blue crab meat
3 tablespoons margarine
1 medium, finely chopped onion
5 tomatillos, husked and quartered
3 minced garlic cloves
3 packages (10 ounces each) frozen
  corn kernels

4 cups chicken broth
1/4 cup snipped fresh cilantro
1 can (4 ounces) diced green chilies
1/4 cup frozen, thawed or 1 cup
  fresh spinach leaves, chopped

Pick through crab meat to remove any remaining shell or cartilage. Melt margarine in large stew pot. Add onions, tomatillos and garlic and saute for 5 minutes. Add corn, 3 cups broth and cilantro. Puree mixture in blender or food processor in batches. Return puree to pot and bring to simmer. Add remaining ingredients and simmer for 15 minutes. Salt to taste. Serve hot with tortilla chips and a small dollop of sour cream on top of each serving. Makes 6 servings.

Crab and Corn Enchilada Casserole

A make-ahead casserole for when only Mexican food flavors will do. Just pop it in the oven, microwave it, or freeze it for later.

1 pound cooked crab meat or any combination of shrimp or cooked and flaked fish
3/4 cup chopped onion
1 tablespoon canola oil
2 teaspoons ground cumin
2 teaspoons chili powder
1/4 teaspoon ground cinnamon
1 can (10 ounces) enchilada sauce

1 can (14 ounces) diced tomatoes with juice
1 1/2 cups grated sharp cheese
1 cup whole kernel corn
1 can (2 1/4 ounces) sliced black olives, drained
1 can (4 ounces) diced green chilies
9 corn tortillas

In a medium-size saucepan, saute onion in oil for 2 to 3 minutes. Whisk in cumin, chili powder and cinnamon. Add enchilada sauce and tomatoes. Heat thoroughly and set aside 1 cup sauce. To remaining sauce, add 1 cup cheese, corn, olives, chilies and crab meat. Place 3 tortillas in the bottom of a 2 1/2 quart casserole, cutting tortillas to fit. Top with half of the seafood mixture. Repeat with another layer of tortillas and seafood mixture. Finish with remaining tortillas, sauce and cheese. If freezing for use at a later date, cover with plastic wrap, then wrap entire casserole in foil. To cook now, bake uncovered for 25 minutes at 350 degrees or in the microwave oven for 15 minutes, rotating the dish every 5 minutes. Makes 6 servings.

Crab and Corn Soup

A wonderful preamble to a special meal or an entree all its own.

1 pound fresh picked crab meat
1/2 cup dry white wine
2 finely chopped scallions
2 tablespoons unsalted butter
1/2 cup minced onion
2 egg yolks

1/2 cup whipping cream
2 1/4 cups milk
1 1/2 cups fresh cooked or frozen corn kernels
1/2 cup blanched watercress leaves
Salt to taste

Pick through crab meat to remove any remaining shell or cartilage. In a large saucepan, combine wine, scallions and butter. Cook over low heat for 5 minutes, then add onion. Meanwhile, whisk together yolks and cream in a small bowl. Gradually add half the milk. Add to onion mixture and stir over low heat. Stir in crab meat and remaining ingredients. Heat thoroughly but do not boil. Ladle into bowls and serve with garden salad and crusty bread. Makes 6 servings.

Crab Meat Stuffed Jalapeños, page 77

Crab Salad With Hearts of Palm

This recipe idea came from Gourmet magazine. I have tried it with Texas shrimp and it is just as good as with fresh picked crab meat. Artichokes can substitute for the hearts of palm.

1 pound lump blue crab meat
1/2 cup lite mayonnaise
1/4 cup chili sauce
1/4 cup thinly sliced scallions
1 tablespoon finely chopped fresh
   parsley
1/4 cup minced green bell pepper
1 tablespoon fresh lemon juice

1 teaspoon prepared horseradish
Dash Worcestershire sauce
Salt and pepper to taste
1/2 cup chopped, drained hearts of
   palm
Watercress or other greens for
   lining platter
Cucumber slices

Place crab meat in a metal bowl and pick through, listening for any shell pieces. In another container, whisk together mayonnaise, chili sauce, scallions, parsley, bell pepper, lemon juice, horseradish, Worcestershire sauce, salt and pepper. Gently fold in hearts of palm and crab meat. Transfer salad to a platter lined with greens, and garnish with cucumber slices. Or, serve in a tomato flower or with a fruit plate. Makes 6 servings.

Texas Crab Cakes

Traditional Southern crab cakes take on a whole new flavor with the addition of pecans and dill.

1 pound flaked blue crab meat
1/4 cup finely chopped onions
1 beaten egg
3 tablespoons chopped pecans
2 tablespoons margarine

2 tablespoons fresh lemon juice
1 tablespoon spicy mustard
1/2 teaspoon dried dill weed
1/4 cup canola oil
3/4 cup dry bread crumbs

Place crab meat in a large mixing bowl. Remove any remaining shell and cartilage. Add remaining ingredients except bread crumbs and stir until blended. Add 1/4 cup of bread crumbs, reserving remaining 1/2 cup. Form the crab mixture into 6 cakes. Place remaining 1/2 cup of dry bread crumbs into flat pan. Dredge crab cakes in crumbs. Heat half the oil and cook 3 crab cakes until golden brown, turning once. Drain and keep warm. Cook remaining crab cakes in oil and serve with avocado slices and lemon wedges if desired. Makes 3 servings of 2 crab cakes each.

Crab and Corn Cakes

Not what you would expect from a crab cake. The vegetables add extra nutrition and appeal.

1 pound flaked crab meat
1/2 cup grated raw potatoes
1/2 cup grated carrots
1/2 cup creamed corn
1/2 cup whole kernel corn, drained
2 green onions and tops, finely chopped

1 tablespoon chopped fresh parsley
1 egg, slightly beaten
1/4 cup fresh bread crumbs
2 tablespoons sour cream or plain yogurt
2 tablespoons canola oil

Place crab meat in large mixing bowl, and remove any remaining shell and cartilage. Add potatoes, carrots, corn, onions, parsley, egg, crumbs and cream. Heat oil. Form patties with hands and place in pan. Flatten gently with spatula. Cook for 5 minutes on each side or slightly brown and crisp. Turn cakes once during cooking. Drain on paper towel. Serve with spicy yogurt sauce. To make **YOGURT SAUCE** combine 1 container (8 ounces) plain yogurt, 1 tablespoon chile sauce, 2 teaspoons minced onion, and 1 teaspoon lemon juice.

Beth's Deviled Crab

From Beth Weekly in Rockport, whose crab recipe file is overflowing! She has easy access to fresh crab meat—right off her own pier!

2 cups flaked crab meat
2 tablespoons margarine
1/2 cup chopped celery
1/2 cup chopped onion
1/2 cup chopped green pepper
6 crumbled corn muffins
1 teaspoon sage
1 tablespoon Worcestershire sauce

1/4 teaspoon cumin
Dash cayenne
1/4 teaspoon thyme
2 eggs
1/2 cup mayonnaise
3/4 cup hot water plus 2 chicken bouillon cubes

In a small saucepan, saute celery, onion and green pepper in margarine. Combine all ingredients in a large mixing bowl. Place in individual ramekins or in a casserole. Do not pack. Bake at 350 degrees for 30 minutes. Makes 6 servings.

Crab Scalloped Potatoes

A hearty baked dish combining crab meat, cheese, and potatoes.

1 pound blue crab meat
3 medium size cooked, peeled and
 sliced potatoes
1/2 cup finely chopped onion
1/2 cup chicken broth

1 jar (5 ounces) Neufchatel cheese
 spread with pimiento
1 cup dairy sour cream
1 teaspoon salt
1/4 teaspoon pepper

Pick through crab meat to remove any remaining shell or cartilage. In a large casserole dish, layer a third of the potatoes, half of the onion and half of the crab meat. In another container, mix together broth, cheese, sour cream, salt and pepper and blend until smooth. Spoon one third of the sauce over the casserole. Repeat layers. Top with potatoes and remaining sauce. Cover and bake at 350 degrees for 35 minutes or until heated throughout. Makes 4 servings.

Crab Au Gratin

Lumpy pieces of white, tender crab meat with breadcrumb topping baked in a rich cheese sauce.

1 pound lump blue crab meat
3 tablespoons margarine
2 tablespoons flour
1/4 teaspoon paprika
1/2 teaspoon salt

1/8 teaspoon pepper
1 1/2 cups thin cream
1 cup Cheddar cheese, grated
1 tablespoon Worcestershire sauce
1/3 cup bread crumbs

Remove any remaining shell or cartilage from crab meat. Melt margarine in skillet and stir in flour, paprika, salt and pepper. Continue to stir until smooth. Gradually add cream, cook and stir slowly until thickened. Add cheese and Worcestershire sauce, and stir until cheese is melted. Add crab meat. Place mixture in a greased baking dish or in individual bake and serve dishes and cover with crumbs. Bake at 350 degrees for approximately 20 minutes. Makes 4 to 6 servings.

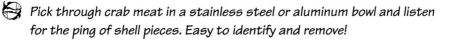 *Pick through crab meat in a stainless steel or aluminum bowl and listen for the ping of shell pieces. Easy to identify and remove!*

Crab and Wild Rice

A shellfish creation flavored with a subtle splash of vermouth and served on a bed of wild rice.

1 pound flaked or lump blue crab meat
1 package (7 ounces) long grain and wild rice
2 cups sliced fresh mushrooms

1/3 cup olive oil or salad oil
1/2 teaspoon salt
1/2 teaspoon white pepper
2 tablespoons extra dry vermouth

Remove any remaining shell or cartilage from crab meat and set aside. In a large skillet or pot with a lid, cook rice according to package directions. Add mushrooms 5 minutes before rice is done. Add crab meat and remaining ingredients. Cook for 2 minutes longer, stirring gently. Serve immediately. Makes 6 servings.

Blue Crab Stuffing

A spicy stuffing full of tender, sweet claw meat is impressive when served in ramekins or natural shells or as a casserole.

1 pound blue crab claw meat
1/2 cup finely chopped onion
1/2 cup finely chopped celery
1/4 cup finely chopped bell pepper
1 clove minced garlic
2 tablespoons chopped fresh parsley
2 cups crushed rich cracker crumbs

1 teaspoon dry mustard
1/4 teaspoon salt
Dash cayenne pepper
1 beaten egg
1/4 cup milk
1/2 cup melted margarine
1 teaspoon Worcestershire sauce

Place crab meat in large mixing bowl. Pick through to remove any remaining shell and cartilage. Stir in vegetables and dry ingredients. Add remaining ingredients and mix thoroughly. Place mixture into shells or casserole dish and bake at 350 degrees for 20 minutes or until golden brown on top and hot throughout. Makes 6 to 8 servings. (Pictured opposite page 79)

 Buy the least expensive market form of blue crab, such as claw meat, for casseroles or dips where it would be senseless to break up large, expensive lumps in the preparation.

Sue's Deviled Crab Casserole

Much creamier than a stuffing, this dish only needs a cool, crisp side dish to win applause at mealtime. This is my version of a favorite of the Casterlines of Rockport.

1 pound flaked blue crab meat
1/4 cup melted margarine
1/2 cup chopped celery
1/2 cup diced onion
1 can (10 1/2 ounces) cream of
   celery soup
1/2 teaspoon salt
1/4 teaspoon pepper

1/8 teaspoon cayenne pepper
2 tablespoons chopped fresh
   parsley
1 jar (2 ounces) diced pimientoes
2 teaspoons Dijon mustard
1 tablespoon Worcestershire sauce
2 teaspoons mayonnaise
1/2 cup dried bread crumbs

In a large bowl, place crab meat and remove any remaining shell or cartilage. Add remaining ingredients except 1/4 cup bread crumbs. Combine thoroughly and transfer to prepared casserole. Top with remaining breadcrumbs. Sprinkle with dried dill weed or paprika. Bake at 350 degrees for 20 minutes until hot throughout. Makes 6 servings.

Crab Meat Ambrosia

A colorful and healthy salad for one of your weekly heart healthy seafood meals.

1 pound blue crab meat
1/2 cup "lite" mayonnaise
1 tablespoon lemon juice
4 teaspoons grated orange rind
2 teaspoons sugar
1 cup thinly sliced celery

1 chopped apple
1 cup mandarin orange slices or
   fresh orange slices
1/2 cup sliced ripe olives
1/4 cup sliced green onions including tops

Place crab meat in a large mixing bowl. Remove any remaining shell or cartilage from crab meat. To make dressing, mix mayonnaise, lemon juice, orange rind and sugar in a small container. Combine remaining ingredients with crab meat. Add dressing and toss lightly. Serve on lettuce leaves, avocado halves or in a hollowed, lengthwise-cut pineapple. Makes 4 to 6 servings.

Easy-Do Crab Chowder

With all the goodness of old fashioned chowder, this creamy blend of crab and vegetables is ready in 10 minutes.

1 pound flaked crab meat
1 sliced medium onion
1/4 cup margarine or cooking oil
1 cup water
1 cup half-and-half cream
1 can (10 1/2 ounces) condensed
   cream of celery soup

1 can (16 ounces) sliced carrots,
   drained
1 can (16 ounces) whole Irish
   potatoes, drained and cubed
1 1/2 teaspoon salt
1/2 teaspoon dill weed

In large saucepan or Dutch oven, saute onion in margarine until tender. Add remaining ingredients except crab. Mix thoroughly and heat, but do not boil, as cream will form a film with excessive heat. Add crab and simmer about 5 minutes more. Serve with sea toast or buttered bread slices. Makes 4 to 6 servings.

Stone Crab Claws

A taste treat gaining popularity. Enjoy crab claws at a get-together where everyone cracks and picks their own!

Crab claws, 1 pound per person
Red Sauce

Mustard sauce

Thaw frozen, cooked claws in cold water or in the refrigerator. To serve warm, steam for 3 minutes. Be careful not to overcook. To prepare raw claws, cover and cook in salted water for 15 minutes. To make **RED SAUCE**, combine 1 cup ketchup, 3 tablespoons lemon juice, 1 tablespoon horseradish, 1/2 teaspoon celery salt and liquid hot pepper sauce to taste. For **MUSTARD SAUCE**, combine 3/4 cup "lite" mayonnaise or sour cream, 1/4 cup mustard, 2 tablespoons horseradish and 2 teaspoons Worcestershire Sauce. Serve warm or cold. Crack claws by holding them in one hand and striking them with a spoon or knife handle. Enjoy by dipping in a spicy sauce.

Texas Seafood Sauces

A trio of tasty seafood sauces to enhance special seafood entrees. (Pictured opposite page 84)

Island Seafood Sauce: Combine 1 carton (8 ounces) plain yogurt, 1/2 cup "lite" mayonnaise, 2 tablespoons ketchup, 1 tablespoon lemon juice, 1 tablespoon minced onion and 1/2 teaspoon celery seeds. Makes 1 1/2 cups sauce. Serve with crab claws or baked fish.

Rockport Red Sauce: Combine 1 cup ketchup, 3 tablespoons lemon juice, 1 tablespoon horseradish, 1/2 teaspoon each celery salt and liquid hot pepper sauce. Makes 1 cup sauce. Serve with boiled shrimp or fried fish.

Chunky Tartar Sauce: Combine 1 cup "lite" mayonnaise, 1/4 cup sour cream, 2 tablespoons each finely chopped dill pickle and onion, 1 tablespoon lemon juice and a dash of pepper. Makes 1 1/3 cups sauce. Serve chilled with baked fish.

Seafood Dips

Seafood party fare to enhance any buffet. Use the seafood of your choice for any of these dips.

Nutty Fish Dip: Combine 1 pound cooked and flaked fish, 1 cup sour cream, plain yogurt or blended cottage cheese, 1/4 cup peanut dust (use blender), 1 tablespoon fresh lemon juice, 3 tablespoons minced onion, 1/4 teaspoon salt. Blend and chill. Sprinkle with additional nut dust.

Crab Meat Guacamole: Combine 1/2 pound blue crab meat, 2 ripe and mashed avocados, 2 tablespoons each mayonnaise, lemon juice and grated onion, 1/2 teaspoon hot pepper sauce and 1/4 teaspoon salt. Mix well and chill.

Texas Shrimp Dip: Combine 1 cup cooked and chopped shrimp, 1 package (8 ounces) softened cream cheese, 1/4 cup each chopped onion, stuffed olives and "lite" mayonnaise, 1/4 teaspoon each salt and white pepper. Garnish with cooked shrimp. Each recipe makes about 2 cups dip.

Spicy Black Bean and Corn Salsa

Good as an accompaniment to any grilled, baked or broiled fish or as a side dish for Mexican food.

2 cups drained and rinsed canned
   black beans
1 package (10 ounces) whole kernel
   corn, thawed and drained
1/2 cup chopped fresh cilantro
6 tablespoons fresh lime juice

6 tablespoons canola oil
1/4 cup minced red onion
1/4 cup minced green onion
1 1/2 teaspoons ground cumin
1/2 cup chopped tomatoes
Salt and pepper to taste

Combine all ingredients in a mixing bowl and chill. Makes 6 servings.

Recipes Alphabetized

Categorical Index

Fish

Holiday, Party Food

Oyster

Epilogue

This book is for my sister, B.J. Reddell Kuehn, who would have thought it was so great that she would have bought hundreds of copies for her friends. She would have been a great supporter and remains an inspiration. And for my other sister, Sharon Reddell Pierce, whose "when are you going to do your book?" kept me motivated. For my parents Anne and Rex Reddell who always believed their three girls could do anything and knew this book would be a reality from the day I said I would write it. For my husband, Ed, and daughter, Dabney, who ate so much fish during the testing of these recipes that they would come to the dinner table imitating fish lips and fins and good naturedly evaluated each recipe with a yea! or a yuk! A special thank you to Sea Grant Associate Director Amy Broussard for her editing and design talents, and the rest of the wonderful Texas A&M Sea Grant group who support seafood marketing and consumer education efforts in countless ways. Their belief in the importance of conveying to you the outstanding benefits of seafood is the reason for this publication.